Biblical Studies in Motion:

British Korean Scholarly Contributions

Hermit Kingdom Studies in History and Religion, 5

Biblical Studies in Motion:
British Korean Scholarly Contributions

Edited by

Heerak Christian Kim

The Hermit Kingdom Press, Inc.
Highland Park * Seoul * Bangalore * Cebu

Biblical Studies in Motion: British Korean Scholarly Contributions
(Hermit Kingdom Studies in History and Religion, 5)

Copyright ©2009 The Hermit Kingdom Press, Inc.

All rights reserved. No part of this book may be reproduced in any form or by any means, electronic or mechanical, including photocopying, recording, or by any information storage and retrieval system (including computer files in any form), without permission in writing from the publisher.

Hardcover ISBN13: 978-1-59689-084-8
Paperback ISBN13: 978-1-59689-085-5

ISSN: 1932-6696

Write To Address:
The Hermit Kingdom Press
P. O. Box 1226
Highland Park, NJ 08904-1226
The United States of America

Library of Congress Cataloging-in-Publication Data

Biblical studies in motion : British Korean scholarly contributions / edited by Heerak Christian Kim.
   p. cm. -- (Hermit Kingdom studies in history and religion, ISSN 1932-6696 ; 5)
   ISBN 978-1-59689-084-8 (hardcover : alk. paper) -- ISBN 978-1-59689-085-5 (pbk. : alk. paper)
   1. Bible--Criticism, interpretation, etc. I. Kim, H. C. (Heerak Christian)
   BS531.B53 2009
   220.6--dc22
                                         2009029939

Soli Deo Gloria

Contents

Reading the Markan Shema (12.29) in Light of the "Exaltation of the Messiah" (12.36)
/Jang Ryul (John) Lee/ *page 11*

Indian Movies and Their Use of Christian Imagery: Bollywood's "Danav" (2003) as a Case Study
/Heerak Christian Kim/ *page 30*

Priests and Levites in Deuteronomy
/Sunwoo Hwang/ *page 53*

Abraham as the Missing Link
/Heerak Christian Kim/ *page 80*

Biblical Studies in Motion

Reading the Markan Shema (12.29) in Light of
the "Exaltation of the Messiah" (12.36)[1]

Jang Ryul (John) Lee
University of Edinburgh, Scotland

I. Introduction

In this paper, I will argue that Mark 12.28-34 and 12.35-37 *must* be read collectively. Some may instantly recall occasions when either passage was preached separately – often detached from its narrative context. Such practices, however, do not correspond to the fact that Mark's Gospel was written as a narrative. Naturally, the original readers would have understood each passage in the flow of the story.[2] Others, on the other hand, may wonder why the case needs to be argued since these two passages are juxtaposed. Juxtaposition does not, however, establish the case because some neighboring passages do not

---

[1] This essay is a slight revision of my paper presented in Synoptic Gospels Section, the Annual Conference of the Society of Biblical Literature (Boston, MA, November 2008). The paper is to be regarded only as a preliminary study which prepares for a more thorough and detailed work in progress.

[2] See below for my discussion of how Mark used formally different materials and formed a narrative structure of 11.27-12.37.

necessarily have any relationship with one other. Even when they do, the degree of their relationship varies considerably in different instances. For example, the juxtaposition of the Parable of the Mustard Seed (followed by an editorial summary) (Mk 4.30-34) and the story of Jesus' silencing a storm (Mk 4.35-41) does not present any specific relationship between the two. Even if the question about taxes (12.13-17) and the next question about resurrection (12.18-27) are related to each other as parts of the same section, a series of questions and answers in the temple (11.27-12.37),[3] understanding one without the other does not seem to be a problem. Mark 12.28-34 and 12.35-37 evince a much stronger relationship. If one passage happens to be read without the other, an important part of the evangelist's message will be lost.

In this paper, I will argue for the collective reading of Mark 12.28-34 and 12.35-37 based upon (1) the intimate connection between the two passages through the notion of "Kingdom" and (2) a narrative scheme of 11.27-12.37 in which 12.35-37 functions as the climax and 12.28-34 as a stepping stone to that climax. I will then discuss the significance of the collective reading. Namely, the monotheistic statement (12.29; cf. v. 32) is to be understood in light of the exaltation of the Messiah (12.36) – who is clearly Jesus in Mark's Gospel.[4] The understanding of the *one-God* is thus further defined by the presentation of the Messiah who "sits at God's right."

---

[3] Mk 12.38-40 and vv. 41-44 seem to be additional parts attached to the main part (11.27-12.37) by a catchword. 12.38-40 is tied to 12.35-37 by the catchword "scribe" and then 12.41-44 to 12.38-40 by the catchword "widow."

[4] Cf. Mk 1.1, 8.29 et al.

Biblical Studies in Motion

My primary concern is to appreciate fully Mark's Gospel as it now stands and how the earliest readers would have understood it. The question of the so-called "historical Jesus," and the issues related to traditions/sources as well as their transmission cannot and should not be avoided. They are, however, not something on which I shall concentrate.

II. Connection between Mark 12.28-34 and 12.35-37 via the Notion of "Kingdom"

Throughout the Gospel of Mark, scribes(γραμματεύς) are constantly depicted in a negative light.[5] There is only one exception in the so-called Great Commandment pericope (12.28-34) where the readers encounter an "unusual" scribe.[6] After a friendly conversation with him, Jesus pronounces to him somewhat enigmatically: "you are not far from the Kingdom of God (οὐ μακρὰν εἶ ἀπὸ τῆς βασιλείας τοῦ θεοῦ)" (12.34a).

There have been various efforts to decipher this "ambiguous" saying, which is likely Markan.[7] A number of scholars have suggested that the saying indicates that this scribe is basically given a confirmation for his successful

---

[5] See Mk 1.22; 2.6-7, 16; 3.22; 7.1-5; 8.31; 9.14; 10.33-34; 11.18, 27-28; 14.43, 53ff; 15.1, 31; cf. 14.1-2.
[6] See J. Williams, *Other Followers of Jesus* (Sheffield: Sheffield Academic Press, 1994), 172-76; E Trocmé, *The Formation of the Gospel According to Mark* (London: SPCK, 1975), 94-99.
[7] The double negative οὐδεὶς οὐκέτι reflects a Markan style; cf. 1.44, 5.3, 16.8 (Taylor, *Mark*, 46).

entry to the Kingdom upon its arrival.[8] Along this line, some scholars tie the friendly scribe with Joseph of Arimathea (15.43) who is "awaiting the arrival of the Kingdom of God (προσδεχόμενος τὴν βασιλείαν τοῦ θεοῦ)."[9] Others propose that the statement has mainly an 'invitational' or 'missional' nature.[10] The Markan Jesus' main focus in announcing such a statement then is not to give a precise account of the scribe's spiritual condition, but rather to recruit him (who may well represent those attracted to Jesus' teaching) to the Kingdom. Another group of scholars, not denying the affirmative nature of Jesus' statement, notes that Jesus' words point out the scribe's deficiency.[11] Although Jesus' response is overall

---

[8] For example, J. Marcus, *The Mystery of the Kingdom of God* (Atlanta: Scholars Press, 1986), 55, 196; V. Furnish, *The Love Command in the New Testament* (New Testament Library; London: SCM, 1973), 28-29 n.12; similarly, M. E. Boring, *Mark: A Commentary* (The New Testament Library; Louisville: Westminster John Knox, 2006), who yet brings partial qualifications to the current state of this scribe in comparison to that of "disciples" (346).

[9] J. Marcus, *The Way of the Lord: Christological Exegesis of the Old Testament in the Gospel of Mark* (Edinburgh: T&T Clark, 1993), 182; Boring, *Mark*, 346.

[10] Trocmé argues that Mark presents this scribe (12.28-34) as an exceptional figure in order to communicate with the group of scribes about the primacy of Jesus as the ultimate interpreter of the OT and the rabbinic tradition, expecting to gain a few of them (Trocmé, *Formation*, 97). See also J. Donahue, "A Neglected Factor in the Theology of Mark," *JBL* 101/4 (1982), 578-81, 594. Donahue relates his "missional" reading of 12.13-34 to his view on the purpose of the composition of the Gospel, that Mark was written after the destruction of the Jerusalem temple with a special emphasis on gentile missions (594).

[11] G. Keerankeri, *The Love Commandment in Mark: An Exegetico-Theological Study of MK 12,28-34* (Roma: Editrice Pontificio Instituto Biblico, 2003), 173-74; John Painter, *Mark's Gospel: Worlds in Conflict* (New Testament Readings; New York: Routledge, 1997), 167.

positive, his concluding comment in v. 34a communicates an insufficiency of the scribe's current standing.

In deciphering Jesus' "ambiguous" statement to the scribe (v. 34a), scholars have often focused on whether the nature of "the Kingdom of God" in 12.28-34 is futuristic, present or even both. If the Kingdom has already come, the scribe's current position seems to lack something. If the Kingdom is yet to come, as the majority of scholars proposes, the scribe is in a good place to be able to enter when it finally comes. The discussion of the temporal aspects of the Kingdom, however, seems to be only secondary because the adverb μακράν in v. 34 is space-oriented and not time-oriented.[12] The word μακράν is used 12 times in the New Testament and always refers to spatial distance without any exception.[13]

According to the spatial understanding of μακράν in v. 34, one can say that the scribe is in a relatively good position but he has not reached the Kingdom yet. There is a barrier for him to overcome in order to make his entry. The evangelist does not tell his readers any more about the destiny of the scribe after this point—that is probably not his main interest.[14] Mark expects his readers not to fill in

---

[12] The spatial imagery of μακράν in v. 34 has a metaphorical nature (cf. Ambrozic, *The Hidden Kingdom: A Redaction-Critical Study of the References to the Kingdom of God in Mark's Gospel* [Washington, D.C.: The Catholic Biblical Association of America, 1972], 179-180). The metaphorical nature, however, does not necessarily eliminate its spatial sense, i.e., the spiritual distance of the scribe to the Kingdom.

[13] Other than Mk 12.34, see Mt 8.30; Lk 7.6, 15.13 & 20, 19.12; Jn 21.8; Acts 2.39, 17.27, 22.21; Eph 2.13 & 17.

[14] Van Iersel says, "After enacting his part he [the scribe] is not mentioned again, as is the case with other characters who have only a walk-on part in the book." (Cf. 12.44; 14.9; 15.21, 39, 46) See Bas M.

the blanks with imagination, but rather to pay attention to the fact that there is still something deficient with the position of this scribe.

Concerning the suggestion that this scribe parallels Joseph of Arimathea (15.32) who waits for the arrival of the Kingdom of God,[15] the spatial orientation of the Kingdom in 12.34 and the difference between the two figures in terms of their association with Jesus disproves such a suggestion. Joseph of Arimathea's association with Jesus appears much stronger than that of the unnamed scribe especially in regards to Joseph's courageous request for the corpse of Jesus and his proactive role in Jesus' burial (15.43ff.).[16]

Concerning the invitational/missional aspect of the statement in v. 34a, it seems that this aspect does not necessarily exclude the observation of the deficiency in the scribe's current position. Rather, these two complement each other since the scribe's deficiency offers a reason for the invitation and the invitation points out the lack in his present state.

The understanding of the statement in v. 34 as above leads to a discovery of the intimate connection between 12.28-34 and the following pericope, 12.35-37,

---

F. van Iersel, *Mark: A Reader-response Commentary* (JSNTSup, 164; Sheffield: Sheffield Academic Press, 1998), 381.

[15] J. Marcus, *The Way of the Lord: Christological Exegesis of the Old Testament in the Gospel of Mark* (Edinburgh: T&T Clark, 1993), 182; Boring, *Mark*, 346.

[16] Cf. Ambrozic, *The Hidden Kingdom*, 179-81, which Marcus neglects while he refers to p. 242 to support his own view (Marcus, *Way*, 182 n. 109). See also J. Williams, *Other Followers of Jesus*, 190-91, who notes a connection between the two figures, yet, rightly distinguishes Joseph from the friendly scribe in view of the former's daring action for Jesus' burial.

namely, the lack in the scribe's current position (v. 34a) can be overcome by the rightful acknowledgement[17] of Jesus' identity as the one who participates in the sovereign rule of God (vv. 35-37).[18]

Psalm 110.1 is, no doubt, the most quoted Old Testament text in the New.[19] In the writings of the New Testament, Psalm 110.1 is applied to Jesus as a scriptural basis for his resurrection, ascension/exaltation, divine authority (in the present and coming eras) and/or priestly office, sometimes associated with Christological titles. In Mark 12.36, it is employed to address Jesus' coregency with God in line with its only other use in the Gospel, 14.62, where the combined use of Psalm 110.1 and Daniel 7.13[20] causes the charge of blasphemy (Mk 14.64).[21] It is important to notice that Psalm 110.1 was not merely quoted but interpreted by various New Testament writers in relation to their understanding of Jesus' identity. As Hay

---

[17] Here, "acknowledgement" needs to be understood not merely as an intellectual recognition, but as a holistic response which involves an action. In Mark's Gospel, the issue of Christology (who Jesus is) is inseparably connected to the issue of discipleship (how to follow him).
[18] Cf. Keerankeri, *Love Commandment,* 174-75.
[19] See Matt 22.44; 26.64; Mark 12.36; 14.62; 16.19; Luke 20.42-43; 22.69; Acts 2.33-35; 5.31; 7.55-56; Rom 8.34; 1 Cor 15.25; Eph 1.20; 2.6; Col 3.1; Heb 1.3, 13; 8.1; 10.12-13; 12.2; 1 Pet 3.22; possibly Rev 3.21. For the conflation of Ps 110.1 with Ps 8.7, see Mk 12.36; par. Matt 22.44; 1 Cor 15.25-28; Eph 1.20-22; 1 Pet 3.22; cf. Heb 1.13-2.9. Only v. 1 and v. 4 from this psalm are quoted in the NT. For the quotations of v. 4, see Heb 5.6, 7.17, 21.
[20] Ps 110 and Dan 7 are the only OT passages that speak of a figure enthroned beside God. It is noteworthy that these two scriptures are interlinked in the trial narrative (Mk 14.62).
[21] Mark does not give any hint that the high priest misunderstood Jesus' response (Mk 14.61-64). The problem of the high priest is not that he has misunderstood Jesus' claim (14.62) but that he has ignored its significance and rather reacted against him.

concludes in his monograph, "early Christians used Psalm 110 to affirm both their sense of continuity with Jewish scriptures and their belief that Jesus transcended Jewish expectations and all human categories."[22] 'Sitting on God's right' certainly goes beyond the boundary of any other Royal Psalms and, according to Hengel, is understood as a claim to share the Divine throne with YHWH himself.[23] Along this line, Bauckham points out that "[t]he concern of early Christology, from its root in the exegesis of Psalm 110.1 and related texts, was to understand the identification of Jesus with God."[24]

Jesus' self-portrayal as God's coregent in Mark 12.35-37, by applying Psalm 110.1 to himself (Mk 12.36), is linked to the reference to "the Kingdom of God" v. 34a. The connection between the image of the 'Royal Rule of God' enclosed in the phrase "the Kingdom of God" (v.34a)[25] and the image of Jesus' participation in the sovereign rule of God expressed through the quotation of

---

[22] D. Hay, *Glory at the Right Hand: Psalm 110 in Early Christianity* (Monograph Series; Nashville: Abingdon Press, 1973), 162.

[23] M. Hengel, *Studies in Early Christology* (Edinburgh: T&T Clark, 1995), 185ff.

[24] R. Bauckham, "The Throne of God and the Worship of Jesus," in C. Newman, etc., eds., The *Jewish Roots of Christological Monotheism: Papers from the St. Andrews Conference on the Historical Origins of the Worship of Jesus* (Leiden: Brill, 1999), 43-69 (64); cf. *God Crucified: Monotheism and Christology in the New Testament* (Carlisle: Paternoster, 1998), 29-32.

[25] On the concept of God's Kingdom as God' royal rule, see J. P. Meier's discussion in *A Marginal Jew. Rethinking the Historical Jesus: Mentor, Message and Miracles* (The Anchor Bible Reference Library; New York: Doubleday, 1994), 237-88.

Psalm 110.1 (Mk 12. 36)²⁶ interlock these two neighboring passages. This offers one reason why these two passages need be read collectively.

Some may object to the validity of the collective reading by maintaining that Christological concerns are not present in 12.28-34. The fact that Jesus is seen to pronounce the person's distance or nearness to the Kingdom, however, places a unique authority with him and is indeed Christological.²⁷ Moreover, the necessity of reading 12.28-34 with the following pericope (12.35-37) collectively reflects the evangelist's Christological concern in employing the Love Commandment passage and its Shema²⁸ as will be further discussed below. The context in

---

²⁶ See F. Matera, *The Kingship of Jesus* (Chico, CA: Scholars Press, 1982), 67-91. Matera argues that the second κύριος in 12.36 (Ps 110.1 = LXX 109.1) is "a surrogate for king" (cf. Mk 11.3) (88). Therefore, in addressing the Messiah as his Lord, David "salutes him as his king" (89). Note his comment on the link between the 'Lord' language and the 'King' language in the OT and Pss. Sol. (88). I do not endorse the entire argument of Matera who asserts that the royal theme penetrates chapters 11-12 and chapter 15. Nonetheless, it cannot be denied that the imagery of 12.35-37, and esp. the quotation of Ps 110.1, has strong kingly overtones. An emphasis on the apocalyptic aspects of the Gospel should not exclude the royal aspects, at least, in this occasion.

²⁷ Cf. V. Taylor, *The Gospel according to St. Mark: the Greek Text* [2nd ed; London: Macmillan, 1966], 490.

²⁸ The term "Shema" has been used by different scholars to refer to slightly different things. For example, Deut 6.4; Deut 6.4-5; Deut 6.4-9; *Shema* as a liturgy in combination of the three scriptures (Deut 6.4-9, 11.13-21; Num 15-37-41); any kind of confession of the *one*-ness of God in the Jewish/Christian contexts. I here limit the use of the term

which a passage is placed is just as important as its content in revealing the evangelist's concern.

Others may point out that the portrayal of Jesus' identity in 12.35-37 is communicated allusively rather than descriptively and, therefore, drawing too much Christological implication from the passage is improper. Of course, from a purely literary-critical perspective, Mark prepares his readers for a more explicit presentation of Jesus' identity in later sections, especially, 14.61-62 and 15.39. Mark's original readers, who are post-resurrection believers of Jesus, however, were likely already familiar with the story of Jesus' ministry, crucifixion and resurrection with some details (cf. 1.1, 14.9, 15.21). Thus the "implicitness" of Mark's presentation of Jesus' coregency with God in 12.35-37 was not all that implicit for them. To them, 12.35-37 does not simply present Jesus' clever scholastic argument against a common scribal understanding of the Son of David. Rather, a piece of scriptural reference to Psalm 110.1 in Mark 12.36 would provide them with a sufficient ground for reflecting Jesus' identity as YHWH's coregent. That Psalm 110.1 was widely accepted by the New Testament writers and likely their communities as *the* main scripture which communicates Jesus' exaltation and participation in the sovereign rule of God supports the position here advanced.[29]

---

specifically to the first and second categories (Deut 6.4 or 6.4-5) with a prior focus on its monotheistic address.

[29] It may be questioned why there is a lack of any sense of objection or amazement in the response of the crowd in 12.37b if Jesus' self-claim was such a "dangerous" one. In reply to that potential question, two things should be mentioned. First, Mark seems to contrast intentionally

Biblical Studies in Motion

III. Connection between Mark 12.28-34 and 12.35-37 within the Narrative Structure of 11.27-12.37

I will now discuss a further reason for the necessity of the collective reading based on the narrative structure of 11.27-12.37. I will first argue that 11.27-12.34 as a whole must be read in light of the Messianic enthronement in 12.35-37 since the latter constitutes the climax in the section. Further, I will argue that in view of the unique function of 12.28-34 in relation to the climactic section of 12.35-37 within the narrative structure of the larger section (11.27-12.37), 12.28-34 and 12.35-37 have to be read closely together.

From the perspective of form-critical analysis, 11.27-33, 12.13-17 and 12.18-27 are controversy stories, but 12.1-12, 12.28-34 and 12.35-37 are not. Mark 12.1-12 does not consist of a question and an answer but is a parable that is a part of Jesus' response to the hostile question about the origin of his authority (11.27ff). In the narrative scheme, 12.1-12 is tied with 11.27-33, thus

---

the receptive response of the crowd toward Jesus' self-application of Ps 110.1 in 12.37b with the hostile reaction of the high priest in 14.63f. The attitude of the crowd will change later under the influence of the ἀρχιερεῖς ("the chief priests") (15.11), yet, at this stage, there is no sense of hostility hinted among them. Second, from a literary perspective, Jesus' self-assertion is made in a veiled way so the crowd's positive response does not necessitate their full understanding of its significance (W. Lane, *The Gospel according to Mark: The English Text* [NICNT; Grand Rapids: Eerdmans, 1974], 439). The lack of understanding in the crowd's part should not be equated with the lack of understanding in the Markan readers' part.

forming a necessary pair.[30] Jesus answers their question by implicitly presenting himself as God's beloved Son (υἱὸν ἀγαπητόν) (12.6) and heir (κληρονόμος) (12.7) in this parable.[31] Jesus' opponents appear to grasp precisely what he meant by the parable and thus become reactive (12.12a). 12.28-34 is a didactic story which records a discussion between Jesus and an exceptionally friendly scribe.[32] 12.35-37 pictures Jesus as posing his 'loaded' question after answering a few himself (11.27-12.34). Basically, the passage consists of a saying with a brief introduction (v. 35a) and an editorial note on the response of the crowd (v. 37c).[33] The arrangement of these formally diverse materials within one section (11.27-12.37) seems very likely Markan. The evangelist ties together these materials to create a cohesive narrative structure.

The narrative flow of Mark 11.27-12.37 reflects a gradual change of "air" in the progression of the questions and answers. The first three questions express nothing but hostility to Jesus. There is no hint of positivity in the attitude of Jesus' interlocutors. The air changes radically by the somewhat unexpected arrival of the sincere scribe in 12.28-34. This scribe receives a qualified

---

[30] The tie is clear in view of the editorial comment in 12.12c: "they understood that He spoke the parable against them." Jesus' attack was thus a *counter*attack against his interlocutors who appeared in the preceding verses (11.27-33).Cf. R. M. Fowler, "The Rhetoric of Direction and Indirection," in W. R. Telford, ed., *The Interpretation of Mark* (2nd ed; Edinburgh: T&T Clark, 1995), 211-13.

[31] One should be cautious about taking contents of a parable too literally. What this parable (Mk 12.1-12) points out, however, seems clear enough.

[32] Taylor, *Mark*, 484; cf. Bultmann, *History*, 54-55.

[33] Taylor, *Mark*, 490.

affirmation from Jesus – he is not far from the Kingdom. Mark then announces the silence of Jesus' opponents (v. 34b): "And no one dared to ask him a question any more (καὶ οὐδεὶς οὐκέτι ἐτόλμα αὐτὸν ἐπερωτῆσαι)." The placement of the silence may seem strange because the scribe in the scene is pictured positively overall (v. 34a) and there was no one else dialoging with Jesus. This silence then seems to refer to the silence of Jesus' opponents in general in the larger section (11.27-12.27) rather than the silence of the unusually friendly scribe. Matthew's placement of the silence after the next pericope is understandable in that sense (cf. Matt 22.46).[34] The Markan arrangement of the silence in the current location (v. 34b), however, has certain significance. It provides Jesus with a platform to pose his own question in the very following story (vv. 35-37)—after responding to a series of questions raised by his opponents and a friendly scribe (11.27-12.34).[35] In 12.35-37, Jesus eventually lays out his own

---

[34] In the Lukan parallel, the silence of Jesus' opponents appears in a similar position to Mark (Lk 20.40), namely, following the controversy with Sadducees about resurrection (20.27-39) and preceding Jesus' presentation of his own agenda concerning the Messiah's Davidic Sonship (20.41-44). In Luke, however, the Love Commandment pericope appears in a different context than Mark and Matthew - in combination with the Parable of the Good Samaritan (10.25-37).

[35] France and some other scholars briefly mention the connection between the silence of Jesus' opponents in v. 34 and Jesus' own initiative in vv. 35-37. None of them, however, really go any further than 1-2 lines of comments. None of them mention the connection between the passages of 12.28-34 and 12.35-37 either through the notion of the Kingdom or through the narrative structure of the larger unit (e.g., 11.27-12.37). Refer to R. T. France, *The Gospel of Mark: A Commentary on the Greek Text* (*The New International Greek Testament Commentary*; Grand Rapids: Eerdmans, 2002); Taylor, *Mark*,

"bias" without the presence of any conflicts[36] since his opponents have been already silenced (12.34b).[37] The question of Jesus in vv. 35ff. then is not simply another question, which equals the weight of the questions in the previous stories, but *the* question which reflects the prior agenda of the Markan Jesus (and the evangelist).[38] The climactic point in the section of 11.27-12.34 is, in that sense, not the weighty quotation of the Shema or the double love commandment, but rather the portrayal of Jesus as God's coregent (12.35-37) - as signaled by the silence of Jesus' opponents (12.34b) and the presentation of his own question that concerns his identity (12.35-37).[39] This

---

490; D. E. Nineham, *The Gospel of St Mark* (The Pelican Gospel Commentaries; Rev ed; London: Adam & Charles Black, 1968), 328.

[36] 12.35-37 is not really a controversy as its Matthean par. (Matt 22.41-45) in which the address is given to the Pharisaic group regarding their teaching, thus clearly constituting a conflict story. Compare Matt 22.46 with Mk 12.34 (cf. R. Bultmann, *The History of the Synoptic Tradition* [Rev. ed; Oxford: Blackwell, 1972, c1963], 51).

[37] Marcus relates the silence in Mk 12.34a to the proleptic presence of the eschatological Kingdom especially in view of *Gen. R.* 65.21 (on Gen 27.22). The silence described in Mark 12.34b, however, is a *forced* silence of Jesus' defeated opponents (11.27-12.27), and not a reverent silence as in *Gen. R.* 65.21. See J. Marcus, "Authority to Forgive Sins upon the Earth: the *Shema* in the Gospel of Mark," in *The Gospels and the Scriptures of Israel* (eds. C. Evans and W. Stegner, Jr., Sheffield: Sheffield Academic Press, 1994), 210.

[38] Even if Jesus technically leaves the answer open in Mk 12.35-37, his answer is already implied in the quotation of Ps 110.1 in a clear enough manner, at least, to Mark and his original readers.

[39] Matera has a similar observation on the climactic nature of 12.35-37 (*Kingship*, 87-89, cf. 68). Matera sees chapters 11-12 as bracketed by the royal entry (11.1ff) and the heavenly enthronement of King Jesus (12.35-37), thus carrying a royal overtone. For Matera's discussion on Mark's intentional structuring of chapters 11-12 and its surrounding passages, see *Kingship*, 68-69. My paper focuses particularly on 11.27-12.37.

observation signifies that the earlier passages in the section (11.27-12.34) can be understood properly when the passage on the exaltation of the Messiah (12.35-37) is in view.

Further, one needs to pay special attention to the role of 12.28-34 within the narrative structure of 11.27-12.37, namely, the favorable dialogue between the exceptional scribe and Jesus (12.28-34) prepares the climactic portion of 12.35-37. Mark 12.28-34 is constructed as the stepping stone to the portrayal of Jesus' participation in the sovereign rule of God (12.35-37). Therefore, 12.28-34, not only by its placement, but also by its special function to bridge to the climatic portion, shows its proximity to 12.35-37. If it is necessary for 11.27-12.34 to be read in light of 12.35-37, the climactic portion, then it is particularly so for 12.28-34. I have shown so far the intimate connection between the passages of 12.28-34 and 12.35-37 and the necessity of the collective reading of these two passages. Now, I turn to discuss the result of the collective reading.

IV. The Significance of the Collective Reading of Mark 12.28-34 and 12.35-37

Some scholars argue that the Shema in Mark 12.29 (cf. vv. 32) functions apologetically.[40] That is, the presence of the unusual figure provides a ground for Jesus to prove his "orthodoxy" and so suggests that Jesus did nothing to deserve crucifixion. The favorable conversation

---

[40] For instance, Boring, *Mark*, 346.

between Jesus and the exceptionally friendly scribe can be understood in that light. Others, in addition to this apologetic point, comment that by the employment of the monotheistic call of the Shema (Mk 12.29; Deut 6.4), Mark intends to warn his Gentile readers against any involvement in the polytheistic cults of their Greco-Roman society.[41] Regardless of the validity of these claims, their common deficiency is to overlook the intimate connection between 12.28-34 and 12.35-37 and to deal with 12.28-34 and its monotheistic statement in isolation from the context.

A more attractive suggestion on the function of the Markan Shema (12.29; cf. v. 32) has been proposed by Marcus. In *The Way of the Lord*, he argues that the evangelist deliberately places the monotheistic statement of 12.29 in order to counterbalance the following pericope which announces Jesus' exaltation.[42] The employment of the Shema in 12.29 is seen as an action of "warding off any misunderstanding of Psalm 110.1 in the sense of bitheism."[43] The evangelist, by quoting the Shema, aims to defend early Christianity from being accused of promoting "two powers" (i.e. God and Christ) theology.[44] To my

---

[41] Van Iersel, *Mark*, 378-79; cf. R. H. Gundry, *Mark: A Commentary on his Apology for the Cross* (Grand Rapids: Eerdmans, 1993), 712-14. Gundry mentions that "[m]onotheism and the subordination of sacrificial worship appear already in the OT. The events of the Seleucid and Maccabean periods plus current domination by Rome make resistance to polytheism a continuing concern in Palestinian Judaism as well as in the Diaspora." Gundry particularly refers to the phrase, "there is none beside you" in 1QH 7.32 and 10.9 (714).

[42] Marcus, *Way*, 145-46; "Authority,"198-201.

[43] Marcus, *Way*, 145.

[44] See A. F. Segal, *Two Powers in Heaven: Early Rabbinic Reports about Christianity and Gnosticism*, SJLA 25 (Leiden: Brill, 1977), passim.

knowledge, Marcus appears to be the only one who has seriously considered the collective reading of the two passages, which are "seemingly contradictory," according to his own term.[45] Even if there is a danger of reductionism in Marcus' reconstruction of the life setting of Mark 12.28-37,[46] his reconstruction does not seem implausible in view of the significance of the charge of blasphemy in a roughly contemporary writing such as John's Gospel (5.18, 10.33) and, moreover, in Mark's Gospel itself (2.7, 14.62).[47]

---

[45] Marcus, "Authority," 201.

[46] Here, Marshall's response to B. Lindars needs to be heard. Marshall critically evaluates Lindars' assumption that the earliest use of the OT in the NT was apologetic more than anything else, in particular, to Jewish oppositions. Marshall pinpoints that its earliest use is not too narrow as Lindars' proposal but rather includes a much wider range - more internal purposes such as the provision of the resources for reflecting the message of gospel and its implication, and also the language for liturgy. See I. H. Marshall, "An Assessment of recent developments," in D. A. Carson and H. G. M. Williamon, eds., *It is Written: Scripture Citing Scripture* (Cambridge: Cambridge University Press, 1988), 8-9.

[47] On the other hand, the fact that Christianity emerged from the matrix of Judaism explains why the former was in a constant communication with the latter, in particular, in its formative stage - either to respond to accusations by the Synagogue or to define the boundaries for its identity and, accordingly, develop its doctrines. Since the early followers of Jesus had to define their identity against the backdrop of Judaism, how to relate their devotion to Jesus with Israel's core confession of faith in the *one-God* would automatically become a key issue (K. T. Tan, "The Shema and Early Christianity" in *Tyndale Bulletin* 59/2 [2008]: 183 n. 9). One should not simply identify the charge of blasphemy in Mark or John with the charge of "two powers" against Christians in the rabbinic literature. Yet, making a general connection between the two would be valid since both concern the issue of Christian devotion to Jesus. It is a mistake to assume that the term, "two powers," was used for one single group. It was often employed to attack various Jewish groups that are not Christians (See Segal, *Two Powers*, 6ff.).

Marcus' interpretative endeavors are to be appreciated, yet not without some qualification. The main problem with his interpretation is that it overlooks the narrative structure of 11.27-12.37. According to Marcus, the claim for God's *one*-ness[48] and the claim for Jesus' exaltation to God's right hand are the two extremes which counterbalance each other. I discussed above that according to the manner 12.28-34 and 12.35-37 are connected and the manner the larger section (11.27-12.37) is 'dramatized,' the climax is not found in the "weighty" quotation of the Shema, but rather in the enthronement of Jesus. Even though the monotheistic confession is recited (12.29) and even repeated (v.32), the prior emphasis of 11.27-12.37, at least according to the text as it now stands, is Jesus' coregency with God (12.35-37). 12.28-34 and 12.35-37 relate to each other not by counterbalancing one another from two extremes but rather by incorporating them with a Christological intent - by first presenting the Shema (12.29; cf. v. 32) and then further defining it in view of Jesus' participation in God's sovereign rule (12.35-37). The employment of the Shema in the love commandment passage reflects the "orthodoxy" of Jesus as a YHWH-revering Jew. But that Shema is redefined by the inclusion of Jesus in the understanding of God (v.36).

If there was indeed a charge of bitheism or something similar to it and thus Mark felt a need to defend the Christian position against the charge as Marcus assumes, the main purpose of the evangelist's "apology" was to show that the understanding of the *one-God* should include

---

[48] I hyphenate this word ("*one*-ness") to preserve the actual term in the Markan text, εἷς (one), as literally as possible.

this exalted Jesus.[49] If the sovereignty of the *one-God* includes Jesus' coregency, the charge of bitheism against Christians becomes ungrounded and thus dismissed. Jesus' inclusion into the divine sovereignty, in that sense, does not violate 'monotheism' but brings its further clarification.

For the Markan evangelist, to love the *one-God* of Israel and him alone (Mk 12.30; cf. Deut 6.5) is materialized through the acknowledgment of Jesus' unique identity. The scribe's positive response to Jesus' teaching is overall commendable yet is still deficient since it lacks a proper acknowledgement of the identity of Jesus. In that sense, the exceptionally friendly scribe is "not far from the Kingdom of God" (Mk 12.34) - close but not there yet.

---

[49] Cf. M. D. Hooker, *A Commentary on the Gospel according to St. Mark* ([New ed.]; London: A & C Black, 1991), 290-91, finds an apologetic force from 12.35-37 in that the passage is employed to answer the question of the role and status of Jesus either between Jews and Christians or within Christian circles. Hooker suggests that the latter would be more likely. It is, however, regretful that she does not take seriously the intimate connection between this passage and the preceding one.

Biblical Studies in Motion

Indian Movies and Their Use of Christian Imagery: Bollywood's "Danav" (2003) as a Case Study[1]

Heerak Christian Kim
Jesus College, Cambridge

India's Bollywood movie industry[2] is a powerhouse film industry in Asia. With about one billion people in India, Bollywood movie industry can be argued to be a major force in the area of film in the world.[3] Interestingly enough, many Bollywood movies utilize biblical imagery.

---

[1] This academic paper was delivered at the Religion, Art, and Culture Section of 2008 American Academy of Religion Upper Midwest Regional Meeting, held in Luther Seminary in St. Paul, Minnesota on March 28-29, 2008.

[2] In contrast to Hollywood, India's Bollywood has been viewed negatively by the state, which tried to control its economic power and cultural influence. This state policy of India is due to Gandhi's perception of cinema as corrupting evil and Nehru's understanding of Indian cinema as tied to modernization. Tejaswini Ganti writes: "Both Gandhi's view of cinema as corrupting, and Nehru's view of film as a tool for modernization have crucially shaped state policy and rhetoric toward cinema in independent India. Gandhi's moralism and nativism and Nehru's internationalism and modernism are present in prohibitive policies such as censorship and taxation and in developmental policies that established a cultural and cinematic bureaucracy to counter the dominance of the commercially oriented film industries" (Tejaswini Ganti, *Bollywood: A Guidebook to Popular Hindi Cinema* <New York: Routledge, 2004>, p. 47).

[3] Nasreen Munni Kabir writes: "Indian films are unquestionably the most-seen movies in the world. And we're not just talking about the billion-strong audiences in India itself, where 12 million people are said to go to the cinema everyday, but of large audiences well beyond the Indian subcontinent and the Diaspora, in such unlikely places as Russia, China, the Middle East, the Far East, Egypt, Turkey and Africa" (Nasreen Munni Kabir, *Bollywood: The Indian Cinema Story* <London: Channel 4 Books, 2001>, p. 1).

Biblical Studies in Motion

And often, biblical imagery is used without negative portrayal. In other words, biblical imagery is used[4] in the way they are used in the Bible without a criticism of the biblical tradition surrounding the imagery or the imagery itself. A good example of the use of biblical imagery in the way of original intent in the Bible is found in the Bollywood movie, "Danav" (2003), a movie by Makrand Deshpande, who adapted his play into a screenplay and directed the movie. Makrand Deshpande is a renown actor and director of Hindi and Marathi film. But Makrand Deshpande is more known for his contribution to Hindi and Marathi theatre, as he has written 19 full-length plays and 12 short plays. In his 2003 movie, "Danav" (2003), Makrand Deshpande utilizes the biblical imageries attached to the Garden of Eden and the Samson story[5] to build his characters and the plotline.[6] To a large part, Makrand Desphande is faithful to the biblical imageries found in the Book of Genesis and the Book of Judges in the Bible. In fact, the imagery of the Garden of Eden and the Samson story is intricately woven into the plot of the movie.[7]

---

[4] T. R. Henn describes the pervasive impact of the Bible: "It is clear that it has been burned deeply into the fabric of the life and literature of the English-speaking peoples" (T. R. Henn, *The Bible as Literature* <New York: Oxford University Press, 1970>, pp. 9-10).

[5] The impact of Samson story in "Danav" (2003) is not surprising since the story of Samson has been an important subject for many films. From 1903 to 1996, there have been twelve films about Samson, four of which were made in the United States (Cornelius Houtman and Klaas Spronk, *Ein Held des Glaubens? Rezeptionsgeschichtliche Studien zu den Simson-Erzählungen* <Leuven: Peeters, 2004>, pp. 228-229).

[6] In this regard, Makrand Desphande can be a part of the trend away from typological to narrative reading of the Bible (Stephen Prickett, *Origins of Narrative: The Romantic Appropriation of the Bible* <Cambridge: Cambridge University Press, 1996>, pp. 155-156).

[7] It is important to understand that the movie maker as an artist has a goal he or she wants to achieve. And every work of art exhibits artistic influences that

Biblical Studies in Motion

"Danav" (2003) opens with Thakur Raja Sahab (Sayaji Shinde) engaged in sword play. His Brahmin dynasty has been marked as swordsmen. Thakur Raja Sahab is a very qualified swordfighter and has the adoration and respect of his friends. Like a typical rich noble, Raja Sahab does not engage in anything but diversions that fit his fancy. Fortunately for his Brahim dynasty, his sword play fits into his program of enjoyment. Thakur Raja Sahab accepts a swordfight with two mighty swordsmen with pervasive repute. Although one of his friends has doubts about his sword prowess and worries for his injury in the sword challenge, most of his friends put their confidence in Thakur Raja Sahab, who accepts the sword fight. In the much anticipated sword fight with a famous sword fighter, one whom he chooses out of two warriors, Thakur Raja Sahab prevails and wins the sword fight. Thus, his ability as a sword fighter is established and his family honor upheld.

However, instead of celebrating in the typical Brahmin fashion for his sword prowess, which was to have sex with courtesans and prostitutes for the wealthy, in order to learn the prowess of the other sword, so to speak, Thakur Raja Sahab deviates from Brahmin tradition. As his friends are frolicking in the river with professional courtesans and learning the art of sex from them, Thakur Raja Sahab talks with a girl who appears with his headgear which he had

---

contributed to its development. "Danav" (2006) can be seen in genre as a legend, not unlike the Samson story in the Bible. For a good succinct discussion of the genre of legend in biblical literature, see Ronald M. Hals, "Legend" in *Saga, Legend, Tale, Novella, Fable: Narrative Forms in Old Testament Literature*, ed. George W. Coats (Sheffield: JSOT Press, 1985, pp. 45-55). See also, G. B. Caird, *The Language and Imagery of the Bible* (Philadelphia: The Westminster Press, 1980), pp. 204-209.

taken off while hesitating whether to go into the water where the prostitutes were. The girl, who idenfies herself as a seventh child who is seven years old, chides Thakur Raja Sahab for leaving his headgear on the ground. Thakur has a brief conversation with the unnamed child while his friends are engaged in the pleasures of the flesh with grown up prostitutes, losing their virginity and learning the art of sex from them. Thakur Raja Sahab, who has not participated in his sexual initiation decides to buy the unnamed girl. This disturbs his friends, who warns him that it is not right to have sex with such a young girl and take her as his wife. He tells his friends that he will not have sex with her until she is old enough and seeks to raise her to be his wife. His father, being a traditional Brahmin, objects to his rash move. Thakur Raja Sahab defies his father and moves out of his Brahmin palace.[8] He places his new wife-to-be in a mango garden belonging to his family and tells her that the garden belongs to her.

As the image of the mango garden is flashed on the screen before the audience, the imagery of the Garden of Eden[9] is evident. The mango garden with mango trees look pristine yet celestial. There is innocence in the garden. There is nothing to taint the garden. Into the beautiful

---

[8] The conflict between Thakur Raja Sahab and his father is indicative of the post-1991 Indian cinema's focus on conflict between individual's love desire and the duty to one's family. Previous focus on conflict rising from class distinctions has been replaced in modern Indian cinema. Likewise, "Danav" (2003) does not focus on class distinction between Raja Sahab and the unnamed girl at all (Tejaswini Ganti, *Bollywood: A Guidebook to Popular Hindi Cinema* <New York: Routledge, 2004>, p. 40).

[9] J. C. L. Gibson describes the imagery of the Garden of Eden in this way: "The Garden is a garden of the wind, a garden of people's dreams, the kind of place they would like this world to be, the kind of place indeed they know it ought to be..." (J. C. L. Gibson, *Language and Imagery in the Old Testament* <Peabody: Hendrickson Publishers, Inc., 1998>, p. 95).

Biblical Studies in Motion

garden is placed the unnamed seven year old girl whom Thakur Raja Sahab had purchased to be his wife. It was a pure love as he was not to defile her until she was of the age, and he was willing to wait for her as she grew into a mature woman. It was a pure love because Thakur Raja Sahab, who could have had the first pick of the best courtesan, renounced his opportunity for sexual pleasure and the proving of his manhood to taken the unnamed child to be his future wife. Thakur Raja Sahab is like the Adam of the Garden of Eden. He was the alpha male, the first in his realm. And the unnamed child was like Eve, who was innocent, and desired to be with Adam. Like the Adam of the Book of Genesis, Thakur Raja Sahab gives the unnamed girl, identified only as the seventh child who is seven years old, her name. Thakur names her, "Lakshmi."

After receiving her name, the movie fastforwards to Lakshmi nearing her sixteenth birthday. The grown up Lakshmi (Sonali Kulkarni) and Thakur Raja Sahab has become lovers. Although the moment of their sexual union, when they both presumably experience sex for the first time, is not emphasized in the movie, their togetherness as sexual partners is clear. In as sense, it is not unlike Adam and Even in the Garden of Eden. Their first sexual encounter is not emphasized. It is presumed[10] that when Eve entered the Garden of Eden[11] and receives her name

---

[10] This is the case with Samson and Delilah. Helen Leneman writes: "The sex act between Samson and Delilah is not reported at all. It is assumed to be the means by which Delilah enticed Samson's secret from him" (Helen Leneman, "Portrayals of Power in the Stories of Delilah and Bathsheba: Seduction in Song" in *Culture, Entertainment and the Bible*, ed. George Aichele <Sheffield: Sheffield Academic Press, 2000, pp. 139-155>, p. 145).

[11] In her targum-like interpretation, Shira Halevi calls the Garden of Eden, "Garden of Delight" (Shira Halevi, *The Life Story of Adam and Havah: A New*

from Adam, that was in effect marriage to Adam and that their sexual union[12] was consummated soon afterwards. Likewise, Lakshmi's entrance into the Garden and her receiving her name from Thakur Raja Sahab was in essence entrance of her marriage with him. Since the first moment of the sexual union is clouded in vagueness, we do not know for certain how much into the marriage they consummated the marriage. But it is clear that by the time Lakshmi is approaching her sixteenth birthday, the sexual union had been consummated.[13] Thakur Raja Sahab was visiting her every day and every night.

Targum of Genesis 1:26-5:5 <Northvale: Jason Aronson Inc., 1997>, pp. 73-77).

[12] Robert D. Sacks argues that sexual union in the Garden of Eden between Adam and Eve was not for the sake of procreation because they were immortal before sin (Robert D. Sacks, *A Commentary on the Book of Genesis* <Lewiston: The Edwin Mellen Press, 1990>, p. 27). While agreeing that Adam and Eve had sexual union in the Garden of Eden, R. Gilboa argues that it was "in order to procreate" (R. Gilboa, *Intercourses in the Book of Genesis: Mythic Motif in Creator-Created Relationships* <Sussex: The Book Guild Ltd., 1998>, p. 103). Beverly J. Stratton agrees that Eve was created for procreation but argues that God seems confused in the narrative: "In the garden version, God has given no command to the man to procreate, and the narrator has given no clues that the man is sexually aware. Of course, God may have just at this point realized that the man could not procreate alone, deemed this infertility 'not good' in terms of God's purposes, and decided to remedy the situation before issuing such a command" (Beverly J. Stratton, *Out of Eden: Reading, Rhetoric, and Ideology in Genesis 2-3* <Sheffield: Sheffield Academic Press, 1995>, p. 36).

[13] Due to India's strict censorship, sexual act is implied rather than portrayed. Lalitha Gopalan writes: "The ongoing negotiations between the state's censorship regulations and film industry, particularly over the representation of the female body on screen, can be formulated as *coitus interruptus* – a cinematic technique that is most visible when the camera withdraws just before we see a sexually explicit scene. In the 'lost scenes' with pastoral evocations of passions – waterfalls, rain, gardens and so on" (Lalitha Gopalan, *Cinema of Interruptions: Action Genres in Contemporary Indian Cinema* <London: British Film Institute Publishing, 2002>, p. 37). Manjunath Pendakur also writes: "Rain also gives the filmmakers the opportunity to explore female sensuality in a way that is allowed by censors" (Manjunath Pendakur, *Indian Popular Cinema* <Cresskill: Hampton Press, Inc., 2003>, p. 161). It is not only the sex scenes that are prohibited; kissing scenes are prohibited in Indian

Biblical Studies in Motion

What is quite strange is that even after Thakur Raja Sahab's father dies and the thousands of acres of his family estate becomes his property, Raja Sahab does not invite Lakshmi into his palace. To be sure, the workers in the field call Lakshmi, "Queen," and recognizes her status as Raja Sahab's wife, but Lakshmi continues to live in the mango garden. Although this may be strange from the plotline of an Indian story, which expects the wife of a Brahmin to join him in his estate, the plotline makes complete sense in the context of Garden of Eden imagery woven into the story of "Danav" (2003). Lakshmi was the innocent Eve before the Fall. She lived in her primitive garden, untainted by the evils of the outside world. Lakshmi is the innocent Eve with a good heart who trusts everyone, including Thakur Raja Sahab, who keeps her imprisoned in her mango garden and visits her only when he feels like it.

And like in the Garden of Eden story, where it is deception and jealousy destroys Eve's innocence, Lakshmi's innocence is destroyed by deception and jealousy. In the Book of Genesis, it is Satan's deception[14]

---

cinema. Kobita Sarkar writes: "Since 'kissing' as one of the adjuncts of a 'foreign' romance, is prohibited, there is a symbolism and interpretation in visual terms" (Kobita Sarkar, *Indian Cinema Today: An Analysis* <New Delhi: Sterling Publishers Pvt. Ltd., 1975>, p. 17). But Sarkar Kobita defends Indian cinema censorship in this way: "In the western cinema, 'romance' is the ultimate substitute for 'sex': an end in itself; visually, sex is reduced to vulgar inanities. The songs suggest a little more, verbally, and the paradoxical result of these tacit omissions is that we have perhaps the most truly erotic cinema in the world. A semi-nude couple in the bedroom leave little for the imagination to work on. The excesses of our 'romance' stimulate the average mind to work over-time and the final result is infinitely more disturbing. The thought of what *could* happen is infinitely more insidious than the certain knowledge of what *did* happen" (Kobita, p. 96).

[14] Kenneth R. R. Gros Louis states that the serpent (Satan) made Eve feel like she was deceived by God. Gros Louis writes: "The serpent's first question to

and jealousy which ends the innocence of Eve[15] and the purity of the Garden of Eden. Satan in the form of a serpent appears to Eve and deceives her[16] into eating from the fruit of the knowledge of good and evil. Satan was jealous that Adam and Eve lived happily in the Garden of Eden in obedience to God who forbade them to eat of the knowledge of good and evil. In "Danav" (2003), it is Thakur Raja Sahab's deception and jealousy that destroys Lakshmi's innocence and the purity of the Garden.

Thakur Raja Sahab deceives Lakshmi into believing that he was bringing a circus especially for her to celebrate her sixteenth birthday. The announcer in the streets proclaimed that Lakshmi and Raja Sahab will be first to see the circus before it is opened to the public in the village. The announcer also proclaimed that the circus was in celebration of Lakshmi's sixteenth birthday. Lakshmi waited in anticipation because the circus was touted to be Thakur Raja Sahab's birthday gift to her, and she really loved him. But Thakur Raja Sahab was thrown into jealousy as the announcer announced that the main attraction of the circus was Danav, who was stronger than

---

Eve plants in her mind the suggestion that God has been unjust, that somehow God has been holding back some of favors. 'Did God say, "You shall not eat of any tree of the garden?"' asks the serpent" (Kenneth R. R. Gros Louis, "Genesis 3-11" in *Literary Interpretations of Biblical Narratives (Volume II)*, ed. Kenneth R. R. Gros Louis <Nashville: Abingdon, 1982, pp. 37-52>, pp. 39-40).

[15] Sacks argues that Eve willfully did wrong rather than fall naively into a trap (Sacks, p. 31).

[16] Sacks argues that the Serpent was motivated by jealousy that Eve had become Adam's primary helper: "Perhaps the serpent, thinking himself the most likely candidate, intended to show Man the foolishness of his choice by causing Eve's downfall" (Sacks, p. 27). Thus, the serpent wanted to eliminate Eve (Sacks, p. 28). Gilboa, however, argues that Adam and Eve were both present when the serpent talked to Eve, but "that the man was a silent bystander throughout the conversation with the serpent" (Gilboa, pp. 104-105).

an elephant.[17] Thakur Raja Sahab, having come from the ruling Brahmin family in the region and being victorious as a swordfighter, did not want to imagine anyone as stronger or more powerful than he. In his jealousy and doubt, Raja Sahab did not escort Lakshmi to the first circus show reserved for him and her. Raja Sahab was so blinded by his jealousy that he had forgotten the reason why he brought the circus to the town; it was to celebrate Lakshmi's sixteenth birthday. Lakshmi could not believe that Thakur Raja Sahab had lied to her and broke the promise, so up until the starting of the circus, Lakshmi believes that Raja Sahab would come for her. But he does not. When the music of circus starts off in the distance, Lakshmi has to face the fact that for whatever reason she had been deceived and Raja Sahab had broken his promise to her. In the movie, Lakshmi rushes to the gate of the mango garden and stands inside the mango garden like a prisoner, holding onto the entrance gate bar. Lakshmi asks the blind gatekeeper to open the gates, but he does not.

Thakur Raja Sahab had always been jealous of Lakshmi's love and of her belonging to him ever since he placed her in the mango garden. That is the reason why Raja Sahab kept a blind man as the gate keeper of the mango garden. Being blind, the gate keeper could not gaze upon Lakshmi's beauty. Thakur Raja Sahab wanted Lakshmi's beauty for himself only. Thus, workers of the

---

[17] Sumita S. Chakravorty writes: "In cinema, strategies of realism and myth are meant to evoke different responses in audiences, to codify, channelize, and diversify the felt needs of people. If the stated purpose of realism is to stay close to 'life,' then the purpose of myth is to go beyond it, to incorporate the unfamiliar and the abstract, to allow the *dreams* of collectivity to take shape" (Sumita S. Chakravarty, *National Identity in Indian Popular Cinema 1947-1987* <Austin: University of Texas Press, 1993>, p. 120).

mango garden were blindfolded before entering the garden so that they could not behold the beauty of Lakshmi. When Lakshmi catches one of the garden workers looking at her after undoing his blindfold, she tells him to stop looking at her. Filled with jealous rage, Thakur Raja Sahab blinds both of the garden worker's eyes on the handle bars of his motorbike. Thakur Raja Sahab could not stand to share Lakshmi, even her appearance with anyone else. Such was his romantic love for her; it consumed him and made him irrational. Thus, when the announcer proclaimed that Danav was stronger than an elephant, Thakur Raja Sahab became jealous of his power and fearful that somehow Lakshmi would love him.

What fueled Thakur Raja Sahab's jealousy and fear was Lakshmi's excitement at the news that there was Danav in the circus. Ever since her youth, Lakshmi liked stories of Danav and even tried to awaken him by stomping on the ground to Thakur Raja Sahab. Lakshmi's desire to see Danav was not a momentary fancy, but a desire built up over years of hearing stories about Danav from none other than Thakur Raja Sahab. Thakur Raja Sahab, who was taken by surprised that Danav was a part of the circus, was genuinely afraid of what Lakshmi seeing Danav would do to their relationship. Lakshmi dresses up every night to go to the circus after the first night when Raja Sahab intentionally does not take her to the circus. For Lakshmi, the main fascination of the circus is the presence of Danav. When Thakur Raja Sahab visits Lakshmi in the middle of the night, seeking reassurances for her love for him, he finds her asleep and dreaming about Danav. Thakur Raja Sahab is thrown into jealous rage and slaughters many men with his sword, proclaiming that he was more powerful than anyone, including Danav. In his irrational state, Thakur Raja Sahab buys Danav from the circus and places him in the mango garden.[18] Lakshmi only wanted to see Danav in a circus show on the first night of the circus from the audience. That would have satisfied her curiosity. But Thakur Raja Sahab, so filled with jeaoulsy that he did not even want Lakshmi to see Danav, now brought Danav into the garden to be with Lakshmi twenty-four hours per day, every day of the week. Thus, Danav arrives when Thakur Raja Sahab is struggling with his personal demons. Ridden with a guilty conscience, Danav goes to the temple of his Brahmin family in his estate and talks with the Hindu priest. The Hindu priest fails to assuage Thakur Raja Sahab's jealous and guilty conscience, so Raja Sahab kicks the Hindu priest out of the temple and locks himself in. Instead of spending time with the woman whom he loved and who loved him, Thakur Raja Sahab intentionally draws himself out of her love zone and isolates her and himself, making both of them vulnerable.

Lakshmi becomes vulnerable to Danav (Aryan Vaid). She is fascinated by his strength, which is supernatural. She is fascinated by his uncouth, wild animal nature, which stands in stark contrast to Thakur Raja Sahab, who keeps up the form of being a Brahmin noble, despite

---

[18] Just like in the story of Garden of Eden, where the serpent was placed in the Garden of Eden by the owner of the Garden, in "Danav" (2003), Danav is placed in the garden by its owner. In both stories, they become the cause for the corruption of the Garden. Beverly J. Stratton writes: "As one of the animals of the field, the serpent would have been made from the ground, brought to the man, named by him, and presumably deemed inappropriate as a helper or partner for the man" (Stratton, p. 41). In the same way, Danav, treated almost like an animal, brought into do work in the mango garden, would not have been thought of as suitable partner for Lakshmi.

his savage acts. Lakshmi finds tenderness in her heart when she sees the powerful Danav flinching in fear at the braying of a cow. Danav tells Lakshmi the story of his youth and how he, not recognizing his own super strength, milked a cow to death. Because of this, his parents kicked him out of their home to live with wild animals. He realized he was stronger than an elephant as he beat an elephant in a fight. It is, of course, hard to miss the correlation with Samson of the Book of Judges.[19] Samson was a man with super human strengths. He fought with animals and beat them with his bear hands. His superhuman strength was recognized and feared.[20] Danav in the movie, "Danav" (2003), is a Samson figure. Lakshmi comes to have a soft spot for Danav and lures[21] him into having sex with her.[22] Thus, Lakshmi plays

---

[19] Irving Francis Wood and Elihu Grant describe the legend stories in the Book of Judges: "Behind these sources must, of course, lie the old oral stories and ballads, local tales of the deeds of the heroes which were later gathered, with more or less change, into the first written accounts" (Irving Francis Wood and Elihu Grant, *The Bible as Literature: An Introduction* <New York: The Abingdon Press, 1914>, p. 129). The concept of oral stories playing a major role is integrated in the story of Danav.

[20] James A. Freeman writes: "Samson demonstrated that the very talents that authenticate an individual, that enable him to stand alone, are the same that prompt a community to seek and destroy him" (James A. Freeman, "Samson's Dry Bones: A Structural Reading of Judges 13-16" in *Literary Interpretations of Biblical Narratives (Volume II)*, ed. Kenneth R. R. Gros Louis <Nashville: Abingdon, 1982, pp. 145-160>, p. 157).

[21] Eve has traditionally been seen as luring Adam into sin. However, Beverly J. Stratton points out: "Much to the consternation of many commentators, who assume its presence, there was *no* scene where the woman lured, tricked, tempted, seduced, or for that matter even said a word to the man, either to command or to persuade his eating. Nor does the man blame her for doing any of these things. What the narrator has told us, and what the man's response to divine questioning confirms, is only that the woman gave fruits to her husband and that he ate" (Stratton, p. 60).

[22] Active role Lakshmi has an enticing Danav to have sex with her stands in sharp contrast to the passive, and even chaste, role that Indian women are to portray in Indian cinema (Shakuntala Banaji, *Reading "Bollywood": The*

Delilah who subdues Samson under her sexual spell.[23] The mighty beast in Danav is tamed in the process of love-making and tender relationship that forms between Lakshmi and Danav. All the while, Thakur Raja Sahab is in the Hindu temple, fighting his demons and his decision to place Danav in the mango garden. Just as the Samson of the Bible had a weakness for women, Danav falls weak before a woman.[24] Lakshmi holds him in her enthrall. When Danav, in his moments of tenderness, confesses that he no longer wants to be called Danav but rather by his birth name of Narayan, which is a name of a Hindu god, Lakshmi feels herself bonded to him and happy. However, after days of ecstatic pleasures and intimacy shared, Lakshmi realizes that she is not really in love with Danav,

---

Young Audience and Hindi Films <New York: Palgrave Macmillan, 2006>, pp. 111-126). Many conservative Indian cinema goers identify eexual permissiveness as an identifying trademark of western and Christian women. Shakuntala Banaji writes: "Western (and sometimes Christian) women were commonly perceived by conservative interviewees as being willing to have sex with anyone, inside or outside marriage, and also as being prostitutes, lesbians or acting in pornographic films" (Banaji, p. 128). The perception of the west and western women has propelled censorship in India to a "double standard." B. K. Karanjia writes: "Film censorship in India has often in the past been charged – not altogether justly, we are afraid – with adopting a double standard vis-à-vis Indian and foreign films. Not justly, because the censorship of films is, or should always be, with reference to the customs and mores of the country of origin and not those prevailing in the countries where the films are shown" (B. K. Karanjia, *A Many-Splendoured Cinema* <Bombay: New Thacker's Fine Art Press Pvt. Ltd., 1986>, p. 49).

[23] Helen Leneman writes: "Delilah is arguably the most famous woman in the book of Judges, her name as synonym for the mature seductive woman available outside marriage, overtly using sexual attraction to entice Samson (Leneman, p. 141).

[24] Mieke Bal argues that abstinence from sex was related to his being able to be a warrior with a legendary strength: "It is clear that his *gibbor*ship largely depends on his sexual immaturity" (Mieke Bal, *Death & Dissymmetry: The Politics of Coherence in the Book of Judges* <Chicago: The University of Chicago Press, 1988>, p. 202). Danav, like Samson, loses his warrior sensibility after sexual maturity.

but with Thakur Raja Sahab. She struggles with her internal turmoil and experiences she has had and tries to come to an understanding of herself, Narayan, and their relationship. When Narayan tells Lakshmi that he considers her like his cow, Lakshmi gets afraid because she realized the Narayan killed the cow that he loved and therefore became Danav, or "the devil." Being confused about her heart and whom she loved, and being genuinely afraid for her life, Lakshmi tells Narayan that she is afraid of him and his strength.[25] Upon hearing this, Narayan proclaims that he will renounce his strength for Lakshmi and his love for her.[26]

At this point, it is impossible to miss the renunciation of strength by Samson in the Bible. It is true that Samson did not say that he was going to renounce his strength for love, as Danav did, but that was what it was in essence.[27] Samson knew what the secret to his strength

---

[25] Danav's life resembles Samson's life, which placed everyone in extreme situations. Marais writes: "Everything which happens in Samson's world is in a larger than life mode; it is a world of extremes. There is little, if anything, in between. Every reaction is an overreaction; every revenge is a massacre; every prayer is a desperate call; everyone is living and acting on the edge. There is no safe ground" (Jacobus Marais, *Representation in Old Testament Narrative Texts* <Leiden: Brill, 1998>, p. 127).

[26] Bombay psychotherapist Udayan Patel writes: "there is an assumption that true love will never be satisfied, it will always be unfulfilled. It's a seesaw between sadism and mascochism where sterility is transformed into a virtue. And screen heroes are nearly always virtuous" (Kabir, p. 32). From this vantage point, both Danav and Thakur Raja Sahab are screen heroes. Neither really finds permanent, lasting love.

[27] Barry G. Webb describes Samson as choosing Delilah over God in his moment of weakness for love: "Samson is portrayed as acting irrationally in the grip of strong emotions. His supernatural strength is the one aspect of his separation to God that he has genuinely relished, but alone with Delilah he sees his strength as the source of all his troubles. He wants to be done with fighting the Philistines and settle down with the woman he loves" (Barry G. Webb, *The Book of the Judges: An Integrated Reading* <Sheffield: Sheffield Academic Press, 1987>, p. 169).

was; it was not cutting his hair. Delilah was the woman Samson, the man with superhuman strength, loved. But it was this woman who was trying to find the secret to his strength that was going to take away his powerful strength. Time after time, Samson lied to Delilah. Thus, when methods for taking away his strength was tried again and again, they failed. Samson lied to Delilah to protect his strength and his life from his enemies.[28] But when Delilah found out that Samson did not trust her, Delilah blatantly complained to Samson that he did not love her.[29] Delilah made Samson telling the secrets of his superhuman strength a test of his avowed love for her. Samson had to make a choice. The choice was either to lie for Delilah and save his power and life, but possibly lose Deliah, or to tell the truth to Delilah and seal his loss of power and death.[30] Knowing that the revelation of the secrets of his strength was tantamount to giving up his life, Samson chose romantic love to his own eventual death.[31] In the same

---

[28] Webb describes Samson as the opposite of what an ideal judge should be: "We are presented with Samson, who is the polar opposite of Othniel: Othniel's marriage is exemplary, Samson's liaisons with foreign women are the reverse; Othniel leads Israel in holy war, Samson is a loner who doesn't even *want* to fight the Philistines; Othniel saves Israel and ushers in an era of peace, Samson leaves the Israelite under the Philistine yoke. And yet the narrator insists that Samson was a judge, and the point is made with particular emphasis" (Webb, p. 171).

[29] Exum describes the women in Samson story as more powerful than men, individually. But paradoxically, on the macro-social level, they are pawns of men (J. C. Exum, *Fragmented Women: Feminist (Sub)versions of Biblical Narratives* <Sheffield: JSOT Press, 1993>, p. 86).

[30] Unlike Danav, Samson knew that Delilah intended to kill him with his secret. Abraham Smythe Palmer, therefore, writes about Delilah that she was "his treacherous mistress, who is also his implacable foe" (Abraham Smythe Palmer, *The Samson-Saga and Its Place in Comparative Religion* <New York: Arno Press, 1977>, p. 129).

[31] Freeman, "Samson's Dry Bones," P. 147.

manner, Danav renounced his strength for his romantic love and sealed his own death.[32]

The moment that Danav renounces his strength is when Thakur Raja Sahab reenters the garden. He brings in modern farming equipment, such as the tractor, to show his strength over Danav. Thakur Raja Sahab proclaims that he is more powerful than Danav. For Raja Sahab, it was far more important to prove that he was more powerful than Danav, rather than to enjoy the love of Lakshmi. Lakshmi confides in Thakur Raja Sahab that she was afraid of Danav because of his strength and clearly shows that she prefers him to Danav.[33] But that is not enough. For Thakur Raja Sahab, he needs to prove that he is more powerful than Danav, to himself and to Lakshmi. It did not matter to him that he won the war on love, he had to fight the little battles to prove why the war should be won by him. Lakshmi tries to set Thakur Raja Sahab's insecurities at rest by telling him that Danav had given up his strength for her. But her intention is totally missed by Thakur Raja Sahab, who does not take her comments as her wanting to be with him and trying to dissuade him from wasting time proving his superiority over Danav. Rather, Thakur Raja Sahab realizes that Danav loves his Lakshmi. And Raja Sahab

---

[32] Narendra Panjwani writes: "Romance in Indian cinema is unfulfilled love; it is love not fully recognized; it is understatement; it is taking a risk that could be fatal. The conquest of anxiety by desire is romance" (Narendra Panjwani, *Emotion Pictures: Cinematic Journeys into the Indian Self* <New Delhi: Rainbow Publishers, 2006>, p. 55).

[33] Lakshmi betraying Danav is akin to Delilah betraying Samson. Both Lakshmi and Delilah saw their target as an "outsider." Freeman writes regarding Delilah's betrayal of Samson: "The conclusion we must draw from these dank examples of alien wives who betray their Israelite groom is inescapable: only marriages within a group can support and protect" (Freeman, "Samson's Dry Bones," p. 158).

Biblical Studies in Motion

surmises that Danav had sex with his Lakshmi.[34] Thus, Thakur Raja Sahab goes on a jealous rampage against Danav. The situation is exasperated by Lakshmi's comments that he is no longer "Danav" but rather "Naryan," which is his birth name. The fact that Lakshmi knew the intimate details of Danav's life makes Thakur Raja Sahab's jealous explode. Instead of spending time with his wife, Lakshmi, after a time of separation when he locked himself in his Hindu temple, Thakur Raja Sahab brings in more modern equipments, such as the crane, to overwork Danav. He want to show Lakshmi and himself who is the boss and who has the power over Danav. Lakshmi, in the tenderness of her heart, tries to save Danav, but Thakur Raja Sahab interprets that as love. Even from his inferior position, Danav is defeating him in love! Thakur Raja Sahab is angered by Lakshmi's interference, which he takes for Danav's victory, and Raja Sahab tries to kill Danav. As Thakur Raja Sahab follows Danav into the cave and slashes with his sword, Danav does not fight back. He has renounced his strength, and like the powerless Samson, he is beaten down with the sword. But unlike the Samson story where his enemies gauge out his eyes, in "Danav" (2003), Lakshmi gauges out her own eyes with Thakur Raja Sahab's sword. The ghastly sight angers Danav. Like in the Samson story,[35] Danav exerts his last strength to kill his

---

[34] Masnjunath Pendakur describes the fear factor in Indian cinema: "A sensual woman is desirable, but if uncontrolled (and not dominated by the man who rightfully is the owner of her body), she might seek her pleasures somewhere else" (Manjunath Penakur, *Indian Popular Cinema: Industry, Ideology, and Consciousness* <Cresskill: Hampton Press, Inc., 2003>, p. 148). This situation describes the love triangle among Thakur Raja Sahab, Lakshmi, and Danav.

[35] Like Danav, Samson stands separated from humanity in his superstrength from his birth. Barry G. Webb writes: "In Samson's case the separation is not voluntarily assumed, nor is it temporary. He remains *nazir* (separate) 'to the

oppressor. And like the Samson story,[36] Danav also dies along with his oppressor, Thakur Raja Sahab, when he brings down the cave with the strength of his cry. Lakshmi also dies in the cave.

Thus, the movie, "Danav" (2003), which started with a story of an innocent garden ends in the destruction of the garden and death of the destroyers of that innocence. The biblical idea of wages of sin being death[37] is upheld in the Bollywood movie. Indeed, "Danav" (2003) is faithful to biblical imageries of the Garden of Eden and the story of Samson as found in the Book of Genesis and the Book of Judges in the Bible. The faithful usage of biblical imagery in "Danav" (2003) is not atypical of Bollywood movies and their use of biblical imagery. They tend to be faithful in the use of imagery as well as in the significance attached in the biblical context.

---

day of his death.' He may wish to be as other men but Yahweh will not let him be so" (Webb, p. 170).

[36] Abraham Smythe Palmer describes Samson's destruction of his enemies along with himself as heroic. Palmer writes: "Thus Samson 'heroically has finished a life heroic' (Milton), and nothing in his life became him more than the leaving of it" (Palmer, p. 187). A pop group named, Middle of the Road, also describes the final destruction of Samson as heroic in their song, "Fable-Abel-Tables." Middle of the Raod describes Samson's final act as: "Samson neatly turned the tables" (Houtman and Spronk, p. 224).

[37] Irving Francis Wood and Elihu Grant write regarding the biblical account of Adam and Eve: "The purpose of the story is found in the prophetic teaching that sin brings suffering" (Irving Francis Wood and Elihu Grant, *The Bible as Literature: An Introduction* <New York: The Abingdon Press, 1914>, p. 108).

Biblical Studies in Motion

Bibliography

Aichele, George (Editor). *Culture, Entertainment and the Bible*. Sheffield: Sheffield Academic Press, 2000.

Bal, Mieke. *Death & Dissymetry: The Politics of Coherence in the Book of Judges*. Chicago: The University of Chicago Press, 1988.

Banaji, Shakuntala. *Reading "Bollywood": The Young Audience and Hindi Films*. New York: Palgrave Macmillan, 2006.

Caird, G. B. *The Language and Imagery of the Bible*. Sheffield: Sheffield Academic Press, 2000.

Chakravarty, Sumita S. *National Identity in Indian Popular Cinema 1947-1987*. Austin: University of Texas Press, 1993.

Coats, George W. (Editor). *Saga, Legend, Tale, Narella, Fable: Narrative Forms in Old Testament Literature*. Sheffield: JSOT Press, 1985.

Collins, Adela Yarbro (Editor). *Ancient and Modern Perspectives on the Bible and Culture: Essays in Honor of Hans Dieter Betz*. Atlanta: Scholars Press, 1998.

Exum, J. C. *Fragmented Women: Feminist (Sub)versions of Biblical Narratives*. Sheffield: JSOT Press, 1993.

Ganti, Tejaswini. *Bollywood: A Guidebook to Popular Hindi Cinema*. New York: Routledge, 2004.

Gibson, J. C. L. *Language and Imagery in the Old Testament*. Peabody: Hendrickson Publishers, 1998.

Gilboa, R. *Intercourses in the Book of Genesis: Mythic Motifs in Creator-Created Relationships*. Sussex: The Book Guild Ltd., 1998.

Gopalan, Lalitha. *Cinema of Interruptions: Action Genres in Contemporary Indian Cinema*. London: British Film Institute Publishing, 2002.

Gros Louis, Kenneth R. R. (Editor). *Literary Interpretations of Biblical Narratives (Volume II)*. Nashville: Abingdon, 1982.

Halevi, Shira. *The Life Story of Adam and Havah: A New Targum of Genesis 1:26-5:5*. Northvale: Jason Aronson Inc., 1997.

Henn, T. R. *The Bible as Literature*. New York: Oxford University Press, 1970.

Houtman, Cornelis, and Klaas Spronk. *Ein Held des Glaubens? Rezeptionsgeschichtliche Studien zu den Simson-Erzählungen*. Leuven: Peeters, 2004.

Kabir, Nasreen Munni. *Bollywood: The Indian Cinema Story*. London: Channel 4 Books, 2001.

Karanjia, B. K. *A Many-Splendored Cinema*. Bambay: New Thacker's Fine Art Press Pvt. Ltd., 1986.

Kumar, K. Naresh. *Indian Cinema: Ebbs and Tides*. New Delhi: Har-Anand Publications, 1995.

Latvus, Kari. *God, Anger and Ideology: The Anger of God in Joshua and Judges in Relation to Deuteronomy and the Priestly Writings*. Sheffield: Sheffield Academic Press, 1998.

Marais, Jacobus. *Representation in Old Testament Narrative Texts*. Leiden: Brill, 1998.

Oommen, M. A., and K. V. Joseph. *Economics of Film Industry in India*. Gurgaon: The Academic Press, 1981.

Palmer, Abram Smythe. *The Samson-Saga and Its Place in Comparative Religion*. New York: Arno Press, 1977.

Panjwani, Narendra. *Emotion Pictures: Cinematic Journeys into the Indian Self.* New Delhi: Rainbow Publishers, 2006.

Pendakur, Manjunath. *Indian Popular Cinema: Industry, Ideology, and Consciousness.* Cresskill: Hampton Press, Inc., 2003.

Phillips, Gary A., and Nicole Wilkinson Duran (Editors). *Reading Communities, Reading Scripture: Essays in Honor of Daniel Patte.* Harrisburg: Trinity Press International, 2002.

Prickett, Stephen. *Origins of Narrative: The Romantic Appropriation of the Bible.* Cambridge: Cambridge University Press, 1996.

Sacks, Robert D. *A Commentary on the Book of Genesis.* Lewiston: The Edwin Mellen Press, 1990.

Sarkar, Kobita. *Indian Cinema Today : An Analysis.* New Delhi: Sterling Publishers Pvt. Ltd., 1975.

Stratton, Beverly J. *Out of Eden: Reading, Rhetoric, and Ideology in Genesis 2-3.* Sheffield: Sheffield Academic Press, 1995.

Webb, Barry G. *The Book of the Judges: An Integrated Reading.* Sheffield: Sheffield Academic Press, 1987.

Wood, Irving Francis, and Elihu Grant. *The Bible as Literature: An Introduction.* New York: The Abingdon Press, 1914.

Biblical Studies in Motion

Priests and Levites in Deuteronomy[1]

Sunwoo Hwang
University of Edinburgh, Scotland

I. INTRODUCTION

The reconstruction of the history of the Levites and the priesthood has been one of the most complicated issues in the history of religion of Israel. Wellhausen's reconstruction of the history of the relationship between the priests and the Levites[2] has been considered to be the only one of his five pillars in support of the dating of P as the latest source in his documentary hypothesis that has not been shaken by later criticism.[3] The main argument for Wellhausen's proposal is that while P distinguishes

---

[1] This is a revised version of the paper, "Priests and Levites in Deuteronomy," presented in the Pentateuch Section of the Society of Biblical Literature 2006 International Meeting in Edinburgh, Scotland.
[2] Julius Wellhausen, *Prolegomena to the History of Israel* (Atlanta: Scholars Press, 1994), 121-151.
[3] Yehezkel Kaufmann, *The Religion of Israel* (Chicago: The University of Chicago Press, 1960), 193.

between the priests, the sons of Aaron and the Levites; D equates the priests with the Levites. The difference between הַכֹּהֲנִים וְהַלְוִיִּם ('the priests and the Levites') in the post exilic literature (including Ezra, Nehemiah, and Chronicles); and הַכֹּהֲנִים הַלְוִיִּם ('the priests, the Levites' or 'the levitical priests') in D is considered to be a key proof for the evolutionary history of the priests and the Levites in which the separation between the priests and the Levites occurred only after the Exile.

The first serious question regarding this theory was raised by G.E. Wright, in 1954, who had a suspicion about the equality between the priests and the Levites in D.[4] After Wright's proposal of the distinction between the priests and the Levites in D, scholars have responded to his intriguing suggestion and debated this issue further.[5] The crux of this issue lies in the passage of Deut. 18:1-8. Particularly, the interpretation of the ambiguous phrase, הַלְוִיִּם כָּל־שֵׁבֶט לֵוִי לַכֹּהֲנִים ('the priests, the Levites, all the tribe of Levi') in Deut. 18:1 is significant for the discussion.

The purpose of this paper is to investigate and clarify the relationship between the priests and the Levites portrayed in D, a relationship which will play a pivotal role

---

[4] G. Ernest Wright, "The Levites in Deuteronomy," *Vetus Testamentum* 4 (1954), 325-330.

[5] See J. A. Emerton, "Priests and Levites in Deuteronomy: An Examination of Dr. G.E. Wright's Theory," *Vetus Testamentum* 12 (1962), 129-38; R. Abba, "Priests and Levites in Deuteronomy," *Vetus Testamentum* 27 (1977), 257-67; J.G. McConville, *Law and Theology in Deuteronomy*, Journal for the Study of the Old Testament Supplement series 33 (Sheffield: JSOT Press, 1984), 125-53.

in the reconstruction of the cultic history of the religion of Israel.

II. THE MEANING OF לַכֹּהֲנִים הַלְוִיִּם כָּל־שֵׁבֶט לֵוִי IN DEUTERONOMY 18:1

Deut. 18:1-8, the key passage for the discussion of the deuteronomic relationship between the priests and the Levites, begins with a clause, "The priests, the Levites, all the tribe of Levi, shall have no allotment or inheritance within Israel." Unlike other instances of הַכֹּהֲנִים הַלְוִיִּם in Deuteronomy, כָּל־שֵׁבֶט לֵוִי follows לַכֹּהֲנִים הַלְוִיִּם without the indication of the correlation between the two phrases. [6] In this chapter, I shall examine four interpretations of the phrase. Since the interpretation of the phrase is closely associated with the understanding of the whole of Deuteronomy and its use of cultic terminology, I shall evaluate views in the following chapters.

1. Appositional relationship between 'the priests' and 'the Levites'

The American Revised Standard Version renders the phrase as "the levitical priests, that is, all the tribe of

---

[6] Although the Peshitta and the Vulgate translate the phrase as 'the priests and the Levites,' as Jeffrey H. Tigay comments, the translation is forced since the phrase does not have the conjunction 'and' in Deuteronomy. See Jeffrey H. Tigay, *Deuteronomy*, The JPS Torah Commentary (Philadelphia: The Jewish Publication Society, 1996), 375.

Levi." In the first place, the translation of הַכֹּהֲנִים הַלְוִיִּם as 'levitical priests' is generally agreed. Syntactically, the two nouns are in an appositional relation, in which the second noun qualifies the first noun.⁷ The consistent lack of וְ between the two words clearly contrasts with וְהַלְוִיִּם הַכֹּהֲנִים in P where the two words represent two distinct entities. In Deuteronomy, as we will examine later, הַכֹּהֲנִים ('The priests'), הַכֹּהֲנִים הַלְוִיִּם ('The levitical priests'), and הַכֹּהֲנִים בְּנֵי לֵוִי ('The priests, the sons of Levi') are used indiscriminately.

With regard to the correlation between 'the levitical priests' and 'all the tribe of Levi' the RSV supports appositional relation inserting the marker 'that is' between the two phrases. In opposition to the translation, "the levitical priests and all the tribe of Levi", J. A. Emerton points out the rareness of asyndeton of two nouns or phrases in Hebrew syntax.⁸ He argues that if the writer had intended 'the levitical priests and all the tribe of Levi", he would have used וְ between the two phrases.⁹ In favor of the equality between the "levitical priests", and "all the tribe of Levi", R. de Vaux contends that in D 'the Levite(s)' and 'the priests' are employed as synonyms.¹⁰ He says that while the entire tribe of Levi is set apart to carry the ark of God in Deut. 10:8, the levitical priests carry the ark of God

---

[7] See Bruce K. Waltke and M. O'Connor, *An Introduction to Biblical Hebrew Syntax* (Winona Lake, Indiana: Eisenbrauns, 1990), 229.
[8] Emerton, 134.
[9] Ibid.
[10] Roland de Vaux, *Ancient Israel* (New York: McGraw-Hill Book Company, 1961), 362-3.

in Deut. 31:9.[11] A Levite in 18:6-7 performs the function of a priest.[12] Furthermore, the fact that the tribe of Levi as a whole is chosen for the priestly ministry in Deut. 18:5 supports the equation of the levitical priests and all the tribe of Levi.[13]

2. 'All the tribe of Levi' as an explanatory apposition to 'the levitical priests'.

This interpretation is slightly different from the previous position in that the second phrase, 'all the tribe of Levi' functions as an explanatory apposition which denotes "the entire group of which one or more representative items have been specified in the preceding words."[14] While the previous interpretation equates the levitical priests with the all the tribe of Levi, this interpretation implies that the second phrase, 'the all the tribe of Levi' is a bigger category than the first phrase, 'the levitical priests.' In other words, though all the levitical priests are out of the tribe of Levi, all the tribe of Levi is not necessarily levitical priests. The implication of this exegesis is that in distinction with P, where the priesthood is only open to the sons of Aaron, D expands the qualification of the priesthood to the whole tribe of Levi.[15]

---

[11] Ibid., 362.
[12] Ibid.
[13] J. G. McConville, *Deuteronomy* (Leicester: England, Apollos, 2002), 298.
[14] S. R. Driver, *Deuteronomy* (New York: Charles Scribner's Sons, 1906), 214.
[15] Ibid.

3. 'The priests' and 'the Levites' as same group working in different times.

Merlin D. Rehm suggests a new approach to this discussion. He states that 'the levitical priests' and 'all the tribe of Levi' are not two different groups living and working at the same time but they represent the same group working in different times.[16] In his argument, 'all the tribe of Levi' is a later gloss which seems to come from the same hand of Deut. 18:6-8, where the role of the levitical priests applies to the Levites.[17] Basically, what he argues is that Deut. 18:1-8 describes the role of the levitical priests in which 'all the tribe of Levi' in v. 1 and 'the Levite' in v. 6 are added as an attempt to give a priestly right to the Levites of the time of the later hand.[18]

4. Distinction between 'the priests' and 'the Levites'

The King James Version shows a clear distinction between the priests and the Levites: 'The priests, the Levites, and all the tribe of Levi' (Deut. 18:1). The first phrase, 'The priests, the Levites' means 'the priests of the Levites' that is 'levitical priests' in most modern translations. G. E. Wright is a strong defender of the distinction between 'the levitical priests' and 'all the tribe of Levi.' In opposition to the indiscrimination of cultic title

---

[16] Merlin D. Rehm, "Levites and Priests," *The Anchor Bible Dictionary* IV, ed., D. N. Freedman (New York: Doubleday, 1992), 303-4.
[17] Ibid., 304.
[18] Ibid.

terminology in Deuteronomy such as 'Levite(s),' 'priest(s),' 'the priests, the Levites,' 'the priests, the sons of Levi' he argues for D's careful and consistent distinction among cultic title terminology.[19] He insists that it is improbable that one whole tribe carry the priestly function in D where only one central sanctuary is assumed.[20] Thus, 'all the tribe of Levi,' which is the Levites, designates not altar priests but client Levites who are mostly involved in teaching ministry.[21] 'The levitical priests' in D is used as same as 'the priests' in P, which is reserved for altar clergy.[22] Richard D. Nelson agrees with the distinction between the priests and the Levites in D though he contends that the distinction is not as sharp as that found in P and Ezekiel.[23] He maintains that 'the levitical priests' are distinguished from 'the Levites' not by genealogy but by function and office.[24] The interpretation of the distinction between 'the levitical priests' and 'all the tribe of Levi' in Deut. 18:1 allows us to divide the rest of the passage into two parts: vv. 3-5 referring to the levitical priests and vv. 6-8 referring to the Levites.[25]

To clarify the relationship between 'the levitical priests,' and "all the tribe of Levi,' the identification of אֲשֶׁר

---

[19] Wright, 328. In the next chapter, the use of D's cultic title terminology will be discussed in detail.
[20] Ibid. 329.
[21] Ibid. Wright accepts G. von Rad's view. See G. von Rad, *Studies in Deuteronomy* (Chicago, Henry Regnery Company, 1953), 13f.
[22] Wright, 330.
[23] Richard D. Nelson, *Deuteronomy*, Old Testament Library (Louisville, Westminster John Knox Press, 2002), 231.
[24] Ibid.
[25] Peter C. Craigie, *The Book of Deuteronomy*, The New International Commentary on the Old Testament (Grand Rapids: Wm. B. Eerdmans Publishing Company, 1976), 258.

in the same verse is important. If אִשֶּׁה means a sacrificial portion of priests, the distinction between the priests and the Levites is unlikely. Since the portion of sacrifice is for priests, not for whole Levites, if אִשֵּׁי means a sacrificial portion of priests, the interpretation of apposition is strongly supported. However, if אִשֵּׁי is rendered as 'gifts' or 'offerings',[26] the distinction of the priests and the Levites is valid. Since in the context of the passage of Deut. 18:1-8, אִשֵּׁי can be translated as either 'offerings by fire' or 'gifts,' אִשֵּׁי *per se* cannot provide a clue for the relationship between the priests and the Levites.

So far I have examined four interpretations of לֵוִי לַכֹּהֲנִים הַלְוִיִּם כָּל־שֵׁבֶט in Deut. 18:1. I shall now examine D's use of 'the priests' and 'the Levites', and then use this examination as the basis for evaluating the four interpretations.

III. הַכֹּהֲנִים הַלְוִיִּם AND הַלְוִיִּם IN DEUTERONOMY

There are five occurrences of 'the levitical priests' and thirteen occurrences of 'the Levite(s)' in Deuteronomy. To investigate whether the two phrases are used distinctively or synonymously, I shall analyze each

---

[26] Richard E. Averbeck, "אִשֶּׁה" *New International Dictionary of Old Testament Theology and Exegesis* Vol.1, ed Willem A. VanGemeren (Grand Rapids: Zondervan Publishing House, 1997), 540.

occurrence through a close reading of them in their respective contexts.

1. Five occurrences of 'the levitical priests': 17:9, 18; 18:1; 24:8; 27:9

> 17:9 "Where you shall consult with **the levitical priests** and the judge who is in office in those days; they shall announce to you the decision in the case." (NRSV)[27]

'The levitical priests' in this passage clearly are altar clergy who work in God's chosen place, as the previous verse (17:8) informed. Moreover, the usage of 'the priests' in Deut. 17:12 to refer to 'the levitical priests' of Deut. 17:9 clearly demonstrates an instance in which 'the priests' and 'the levitical priests' are used synonymously.

> 17:18 "When he has taken the throne of his kingdom, he shall have a copy of this law written for him in the presence of **the levitical priests**."

This passage requires the king of Israel to read the law which is provided by the levitical priests. To identify the 'the levitical priests' in this passage, Deut. 31:9-13 is helpful, where 'the priests, the sons of Levi' received the

---

[27] Hereafter, the NRSV translation is used.

law from Moses so that they may read it before the people of God. The same expression is used in both passages, Deut. 17:19 and 31:12, in defining the purpose of the reading of the law: "To learn to fear the Lord your God and to observe diligently all the words of this law." This passage confirms that 'the levitical priests' and 'the priests, the sons of Levi' are used synonymously.

> 18:1 "**The levitical priests**, the whole tribe of Levi, shall have no allotment or inheritance within Israel. They may eat the sacrifices that are the LORD's portion."

The description of the priesthood and priestly due in the following verses 3-5 clearly affirms that 'the levitical priests' in verse 1 are 'the priests' in verse 3.

> 24:8 "Guard against an outbreak of a leprous skin disease by being very careful; you shall carefully observe whatever **the levitical priests** instruct you..."

'The levitical priests' in this passage are synonymous with 'the priests.' As Wright points out, in P the priests, who are Aaron and the descendants of Aaron, instruct for a leprous disease (Lev. 13:2).[28] Since this passage concerns the same issue we can infer that 'the levitical priests' refers to 'the priests.'

---

[28] Wright, 327.

> 27:9 "Then Moses and **the levitical priests** spoke to all Israel, saying: Keep silence and hear, O Israel! This very day you have become the people of the LORD..."

This passage is a part of the scene where Moses and the levitical priests are teaching and blessing the two groups of twelve tribes after the Israelites crossed the Jordan. As Joshua 8:30-35, the fulfillment of Moses' commandment, portrays, the tribe of Levi belongs to one of the two groups and Moses and the levitical priests are speaking to the Israelites. In the Joshua passage, 'the levitical priests' are the priestly group who are distinguished from the tribe of Levi. Thus, 'the Levites' who declare to all the Israelites in Deut. 27:14 are the priests.

Through the examination of the five occurrences of 'the levitical priests' in Deuteronomy, it is known that 'the levitical priests' refers to 'the priests' who are a select group out of the tribe of Levi. There is no indication that 'the levitical priests' represent the Levites as a whole.

The two occurrences of 'the levitical priests' in the Deuteronomistic history (Josh. 3:3; 8:33) also reveal that 'the levitical priests' designates priests who are not synonymous to the whole tribe of Levi but rather a selected group out of the tribe of Levi as in Deuteronomy. In Joshua 3:3,

> "And commanded the people, "When you see the ark of

> the covenant of the LORD your God being carried by **the levitical priests**....."

'The levitical priests' are clearly referring to the same priests as in Joshua 3:6. 'The levitical priests' in Josh. 8:33 were already dealt with in the investigation of the passage of Deut. 27:9, which indicates that 'the levitical priests' are a priest group.

The two occurrences of 'the levitical priests' in Joshua are associated with the job of carrying the ark of the covenant. Interestingly, in Deuteronomy, there is a passage in which 'the Levites' take the job of carrying the ark of the covenant:

> "Moses commanded the Levites who carried the ark of the covenant of the LORD..." (Deut. 31:25).

This passage is used to support the equation between the priests and the Levites in Deuteronomy.[29] However, Abba convincingly refutes the equation between the priests and the Levites by assigning the job to either the priests or the Levites based on ceremonial situations.

> "It is legitimate to seek clarification of this question in the larger Deuteronomic corpus of Deuteronomy to 2 Kings...it can merely be stated that there are grounds for the claim that they

---
[29] de Vaux, 362-3.

provide some evidence that in the period of the conquest and the early monarchy the carrying the ark was undertaken, on different occasions, by two distinct orders of cultic personnel, and that which of these carried the ark depended upon the nature of the occasion. The crossing of the Jordan, the ceremony at Mount Gerizim and Mount Ebal, and bringing the ark into Solomon's temple were all occasions of high ceremonial, and at these times the ark is said to have been carried by the priests. On the other hand, the ark sent back by the Philistines on its cart arrived at Bethshemesh quite unexpectedly while harvest was going on; and its appearance with David outside Jerusalem at the time of Absalom's revolt was in connection with a sudden and unobtrusive flight from the city. It is not without significance that it is on these unceremonial occasions that the Levites are said to have carried the ark. .. The references in Deut. 31 to the priests carrying the ark (v. 9) and the Levites as its bearers (vv. 25-6) are to be seen in this context of the whole corpus of the Deuteronomistic history."[30]

---

[30] Abba, 261.

Besides Deuteronomy and the Deuteronomistic history, 'the levitical priests' occurs four times in the rest of the Hebrew Bible: Jeremiah 33:18; Ezekiel 43:19; 44:15; 2 Chronicles 23:18. These references to 'the levitical priests' are also synonymous with 'the priests.'

2. Thirteen occurrences of 'the Levite(s)' in Deuteronomy

In Deuteronomy 'the Levite(s)' alone occurs thirteen times: 12:12, 18, 19; 14:27, 29; 16: 11, 14; 18:6; 26:11, 12, 13; 27:14; 31:5. Investigating the thirteen instances of 'the Levite(s)' will help clarify the issue of distinction or equation between the priests and the Levites in Deuteronomy. Out of the 13 occurrences, ten clearly designate the Levites, who, without property, are dependent on the generosity of the landowners to make their living. Clearly, there is no trace of priestly roles in these occurrences.

> 12:12 "And you shall rejoice before the LORD your God, you together with your sons and your daughters, your male and female slaves, and **the Levites** who reside in your towns since they have no allotment or inheritance with you."

> 12:18, 19 "These you shall eat in the presence of the LORD your God ... you together with your son and your daughter,

your male and female slaves, and **the Levites** resident in your towns ... Take care that you do not neglect **the Levite**..."

14:27 "As for **the Levites** resident in your towns, do not neglect them, because they have no allotment or inheritance with you."

14:29 "**The Levites**, because they have no allotment or inheritance with you, as well as the resident aliens, the orphans, and the widows in your towns..."

16:11 "Rejoice before the LORD your God-- you and your sons and your daughters, your male and female slaves, **the Levites** resident in your towns, as well as the strangers, the orphans, and the widows who are among you..."

16:14 "Rejoice during your festival, you and your sons and your daughters, your male and female slaves, as well as **the Levites**, the strangers..."

26:11, 12, 13 "Then you, together with **the Levites** and the aliens ... When you have finished paying all the tithe of your produce in the third year giving it to **the Levites**, the aliens, the orphans ...then you shall say before the LORD your God: "I have removed the sacred portion from the house, and I have given it to **the Levites**..."

The debated passages are the other occurrences: 18:6; 27:14; 31:25.

For the passage of 31:25, we saw earlier that in the corpus of Deuteronomy and the Deuteronomistic history, based on the significance of the ceremonial character, either the priests or the Levites are assigned to be bearers of the ark of the covenant of the Lord. Thus, 'the Levites' in this passage does not have to be the priests of the tribe of Levi.

The only case in Deuteronomy in which 'The Levites' appears to refer to the priests occurs in 27:14:

> 27:14 "Then **the Levites** shall declare in a loud voice to all the Israelites..."

As we saw above, in the identification of 'the levitical priests' of Deut. 27:9, 'the Levites' in Deut. 27:14 are not a tribe of Levi that already belongs to one group of six tribes standing on Mount Gerizim but a small part of the tribe of Levi, the priests as confirmed in Joshua 8:33:

> "All Israel,... stood on opposite sides of the ark in front of the levitical priests... half of them in front of Mount Gerizim and half of them in front of Mount Ebal, as Moses the servant of the LORD had commanded at the first, that they should bless the people of Israel."

Since the identification of 'a Levite' in Deut. 18:6 is a highly complicated and crucial issue, I shall closely examine it in the next chapter.

IV. הַלֵוִי IN DEUTERONOMY 18:6

> Deut. 18:6 "If **a Levite** leaves any of your towns, from wherever he has been residing in Israel, and comes to the place that the LORD will choose and he may come whenever he wishes."

The issue of this chapter is to find out whether 'a Levite' in Deut. 18:6 is synonymous to a priest or a non-priestly Levite. Wellhausen understands this passage in direct connection to Josiah's reform of 2 Ki. 23:9: "The priests of the high places, however, did not come up to the altar of the LORD in Jerusalem, but ate unleavened bread among their kindred."[31]

In his view, 'a Levite' in Deut. 18:6 is a priest of high places who is deprived of his livelihood by the centralization of the cult.[32] Although the right of a country

---

[31] Wellhausen, 146-7.
[32] Ibid.

priest to be a priest of Jerusalem was maintained, this legislation failed in reality because of 'the kindred' (the Zadokites), who did not allow a country priest to be an altar clergy in Jerusalem.[33]

However, the simple connection between 'a Levite' of Deut. 18:6 and a country priest of 2 Ki. 23:9 produces some problems. Most of all, it is unlikely that Deuteronomy, which emphasizes the centrality of worship in opposition to worship of high places, would embrace the priests of high places.[34] Furthermore, while the priests of 2 Ki. 23:9 are viewed in the light of cultic contamination that makes them unfit for the ministry in Jerusalem, 'a Levite' in Deut. 18:6 is portrayed as a non-priestly Levite who desires to be a priest.[35] The move of a Levite in Deut. 18:6 is spontaneous and voluntary whereas the move of the priests in 2 Ki. 23:9 is forced.[36]

We find another clue against the connection between 'a Levite' of Deut. 18:6 and 'the priests' of 2 Ki. 23:9 from a careful exegesis of Deut. 18:6-8. There are two possible translations of Deut 18:6-8.

The first way of translation views the passage as two sentences: "[6] If a Levite leaves any of your towns... [7] then he may minister in the name of the LORD his God,... [8] They shall have equal portions to eat..." V. 6, which is protasis and v. 7, which is apodosis constitute one sentence

---

[33] Ibid.

[34] J. G. McConville, "Priests and Levites in Ezekiel: A Crux in the Interpretation of Israel's History," *Tyndale Bulletin* 34 (1983), 6.
[35] A. D. H. Mayes, *Deuteronomy*, New Century Bible (London: Marshall, Morgan & Scott 1979), 278-9.
[36] Nelson, 232.

and v. 8 is the second sentence. This translation seems to reflect the interests of 2 Ki. 23:9, which is concerned with the permission of the priest of high places to serve in Jerusalem. The LXX and the Revised Standard Version follow the first translation.

The second way of translation regards the passage of Deut. 18:6-8 as one sentence. "⁶ If a Levite leaves any of your towns... ⁷ and if he may minister in the name of the LORD his God,... ⁸ then, they shall have equal portions to eat..." In this translation, v.7 is the second protasis and v. 8 is the apodosis of the vv. 6-7. When we render the passage this way, the focus is very different from 2 Ki. 23:9. The focus of the second translation is not the permission of Levite's ministry in the central sanctuary but the proper portions due for a Levite. The New English Bible and S. R. Driver[37] follow the second option which is preferable both syntactically and semantically. Syntactically, it is natural to break the sentence where waw-consecutive ceases and simple imperfect appears[38]:

וְכִי־יָבֹא ... וּבָא ... וְשֵׁרֵת ... // יֹאכֵלוּ
[apodosis]　　　　　　　　　　[protasis]

Semantically, since the context of the passage is concerned with portions due for the priests and the Levites, it is more plausible to focus on the portion of a Levite. Consequently, when the

---

[37] Driver, 217.
[38] R. K. Duke, "The Portion of the Levite: Another Reading of Deuteronomy 18:6-8," *Journal of Biblical Literature* 106 (1987), 196-8.

second translation is preferred, the connection between 'a Levite' in Deut. 18:6 and 'the priests' of 2 Ki. 23:9 is weakened.

One issue to consider for the identification of 'a Levite' in Deut. 18:6 is the terminologies used to describe the role of 'a Levite.' According to Driver, וְשֵׁרֵת בְּשֵׁם יְהוָה ('and minister in the name of YHWH'), and הָעֹמְדִים...לִפְנֵי יְהוָה ('who stand before YHWH'), which are distinctively priestly terms, indicate that 'a Levite' in the passage is a priest.[39] However, concordance data do not support his claim. The phrase,

שרת ...יהוה ('to minister to YHWH')

occurs with not only the priests but also the Levites in cultic setting. There are 13 occurrences of 'ministering to Yahweh' in relation to the Levites in the Hebrew Bible.[40] In Deuteronomy, 'to minister to YHWH' occurs with both the Levites (Deut. 10:8) and priests (Deut. 17:12). Likewise, the phrase,

עמד.....לפני יהוה (to stand before YHWH), is

hardly to be considered as a distinctive phrase only for the priests. This phrase appears with Levites in Deut. 10:8 and other places such as Numbers 16:9; 2 Chronicles 19:11 and Ezekiel 44:11.

In the light of the distinction between the priests and the Levites, we see that in Deut. 18:7, 'a Levite' who comes to the chosen place

---

[39] Driver, 123.
[40] Abba, 265.

ministers...not 'like all his fellow-levitical priests' but 'like all his fellow-Levites.'[41]

Since there is no conclusive proof for the equation of 'a Levite' of Deut. 18:6 with 'a priest,' we can understand Deut. 18:6-8 to mean that when a Levite comes to God's chosen place to worship, he has a right to receive his portion by doing the job not of a priest but rather of a Levite who is a non-priestly Levite. There are many aspects of ministry for the tribe of Levi and one of them is sacrificial offerings assigned to the levitical priests.[42]

The examination of 13 instances of 'the Levite(s)' alone in Deuteronomy shows that there is only one clear exception, Deut. 27:14, in which 'the Levites' means the priests. Out of the 12 occurrences, 11 occurrences of the Levites, except for 'a Levite' of Deut. 18:6, clearly designate the non-priestly Levites. I have shown that the attempts to equate the 'Levite' of Deut. 18:6 with a priest are unsuccessful. Notwithstanding Deut. 27:14, when the general consistency of Deuteronomy's careful choice between 'the priests' and 'the Levites' is considered, 'a Levite' of Deut. 18:6 as a non-priestly Levite is preferable.

This identification of 'a Levite' in Deut. 18:6 provides a clue for the structure of Deut. 18:1-8 and the relationship between 'the levitical priests'

---

[41] Ibid.
[42] J. A. Thompson, *Deuteronomy* (Downers Grove: Inter-Varsity Press, 1974), 207.

and 'all the tribe of Levi' in Deut. 18:1. Deut. 18:1-8 is divided into three parts:
vv. 1-2 for all Levites, vv. 3-5 for the levitical priests, vv. 6-8 for the non-priestly Levites. 'The levitical priests' and 'all the tribe of Levi' represent not the same entity but different two entities that correspond to the priests' portion in vv. 3-5 and the Levites' portion in vv. 6-8 respectively.

V. CONCLUSION

A crucial issue in determining the relationship between the priests and the Levites in D is the interpretation of 'The levitical priests, all the tribe of Levi' in Deuteronomy 18:1. For the interpretation, an examination of five occurrences of 'the levitical priests' and thirteen occurrences of 'the Levite(s)' reveals that all occurrences of 'the levitical priests' refer to priests and the twelve occurrences of 'the Levite(s)' refer to non-priestly Levite(s). Although there is one clear exception in Deut. 27:14 where 'the Levites means the priests, I have shown that Deuteronomy carefully differentiates 'the priests' from 'the Levites.'

Particularly, in the case of 'a Levite' in Deut. 18:6, which is important for the understanding of the ambiguous phrase of Deut. 18:1, no conclusive arguments for the equation between the priests and the Levites are proposed. The terminology of the 'minister to YHWH,' and 'stand before YHWH' are cited for the ministry of the Levites as well as the priests in Deuteronomy and other books of the Hebrew Bible. The attempt to connect the priests of high places of 2 Ki. 23:8-9 in Josiah's reform to 'a Levite' in Deut. 18:6-8 is not persuasive. In addition, in Deuteronomy and the Deuteronomistic history, the job of 'carrying the ark of the covenant of YHWH' is done by not only the priests but also the Levites. Since Deuteronomy's careful distinction between the priest and the Levites is affirmed and there is no determinative argument for the equation of 'a Levite' of Deut. 18:6 with a priest, it is more natural and preferable to understand 'a Levite' as a non-priestly Levite.

This exegesis sheds light on the interpretation of 'the levitical priests, all the tribe of Levi' in 18:1. When 'a Levite' of v. 6 corresponds to the 'all the tribe of Levi,' 'the levitical priests' is to be understood not appositionally but distinctively from 'all the tribe of Levi.' Thus among the four suggestions of the phrase in chapter 1, the distinctive interpretation between 'the levitical priests' and 'all the tribe of Levi' is preferable to the other three approaches (apposition, explanatory apposition, same group in different period) that view the two groups in appositional relation.

The argument for the equation between the priests and the Levites based on the phrase, 'the priests, the Levite,' which is 'the levitical priests' compared with P's phrase 'the priests and the Levites' produces a fallacy. 'The levitical priests' in D is about the priests not the Levites while 'the priests and the Levites' is about both the priests and the Levites. The right comparison should be 'the levitical priests and the Levites' of D and 'the priests and the Levites' in P. When this distinction is made between the priests and the Levites in D as well as P, Wellhausen's pillar of 'the priests and the Levites' no longer appears to be robust.

WORKS CITED

Abba, R. "Priests and Levites in Deuteronomy," *Vetus Testamentum* 27 (1977): 257-67.

Averbeck, Richard E. "אָשָׁם" *New International Dictionary of Old Testament Theology and Exegesis* vol.1, ed. Willem A. VanGemeren. (Grand Rapids: Zondervan, 1997), pp. 540-549.

Craigie, Peter C. *The Book of Deuteronomy*, The New International Commentary on the Old Testament. (Grand Rapids: Wm. B. Eerdmans Publishing Company, 1976.)

Driver, S. R. *Deuteronomy*. (New York: Charles Scribner's Sons, 1906.)

Duke, R. K. "The Portion of the Levite: Another Reading of Deuteronomy 18:6-8," *Journal of Biblical Literature* 106 (1987), 193-201.

Emerton, J. A. "Priests and Levites in Deuteronomy: An Examination of Dr. G.E. Wright's Theory," *Vetus Testamentum* 12 (1962): 129-38.

McConville, J. G. "Priests and Levites in Ezekiel: A Crux in the Interpretation of Israel's History," *Tyndale Bulletin* 34 (1983), 3-31.

_____. *Law and Theology in Deuteronomy*, Journal for the Study of the Old Testament Supplement series 33. (Sheffield: JSOT Press, 1984.)

_____. *Deuteronomy*. (Leicester, England: Apollos, 2002.)

Mayes, A. D. H. *Deuteronomy*, New Century Bible. (London: Marshall, Morgan & Scott 1979.)

Nelson, Richard D. *Deuteronomy*, Old Testament Library. (Louisville: Westminster John Knox Press, 2002.)

Kaufmann, Yehezkel. *The Religion of Israel*. (Chicago: The University of Chicago Press, 1960.)

Rad, G. von. *Studies in Deuteronomy*. (Chicago: Henry Regnery Company, 1953.)

Rehm, M. D. "Levites and Priests," *The Anchor Bible Dictionary* IV, ed. D. N. Freedman. (New York: Doubleday, 1992), pp. 297-310.

Thompson, J. A. *Deuteronomy*. (Downers Grove: Inter-Varsity Press, 1974.)

Tigay, H. Jeffrey. *Deuteronomy*, The JPS Torah Commentary. (Philadelphia: The Jewish Publication Society, 1996.)

Vaux, R. de. *Ancient Israel*. (New York: McGraw-Hill Book Company, 1961.)

Waltke Bruce K. and O'Connor, M. *An Introduction to Biblical Hebrew Syntax*. (Winona Lake, Indiana: Eisenbraun's, 1990.)

Wellhausen, Julius, *Prolegomena to the History of Israel*. (Atlanta: Scholars Press, 1994.)

Wright, G. Ernest. "The Levites in Deuteronomy," *Vetus Testamentum* 4 (1954): 325-330.

Biblical Studies in Motion

Abraham as the Missing Link[1]

Heerak Christian Kim
Jesus College, Cambridge

The Abrahamic Covenant[2] and Genesis 15 and 17 have made Abraham a central figure in the history of Biblical interpretation for thousands of years. Abraham has inspired commentaries and creative writing not only in the post-Biblical period, but within the Biblical period and among the intertestamental literary works. But in the New Testament, Abraham functions as the Missing Link that justifies Christianity, rather than reaffirming the covenant community of the Abrahamic Covenant. This was made

---

[1] This academic paper was delivered at the Genesis and Christian Theology Conference, held at the University of St. Andrews in Scotland on July 14-18, 2009.

[2] Gerhard Von Rad argues that the covenant is a testimony to the tradition about the patriarchs. Von Rad states: "Abraham, Isaac, and Jacob were the first such recipients of revelation and the founders of the cult of the God of the fathers" (Gerhard Von Rad, *Genesis: A Commentary* [Philadelphia: The Westminster Press, 1972], p. 189). The Abrahamic tradition and the covenant was carefully preserved as relevant to Israelites and the Jews. The early Christians were going against the heart of Judaism by arguing that the Abrahamic tradition was not meant to be hereditary, but rather spiritual and faith-based.

necessary[3] not only because of the Gentile mission, but also because of the outsider status of the leaders of early Christian communities[4] who could not claim hereditary[5]

---

[3] Jerome Murphy-O'Connor argues that political factors impacted the decision of James, the brother of Jesus, to allow Gentiles not to be circumcised. Jews were undergoing persecution, both political and social, such as Jews being expelled from Rome by Emperor Tibrius and Samaritans slaughtering Galilean Jews in 51 AD. Thus, James thought that it was better for Gentile converts to Christianity not to identify themselves with Jews (Jerome Murphy-O'Connor, *Paul: His Story* [Oxford: Oxford University Press, 2004], pp. 104-105).

[4] Gerd Luedemann warns against overemphasis on "Jewish Christianity" that marked much of French and German scholarship in the late 19th century and early 20th century. Luedemann criticizes: "These essays, all written by followers of Daniélou, have a common denominator in that they all speak of Jewish Christianity wherever they find Christian texts that make use of ideas of Jewish origin. But such a concept of Jewish Christianity is too broad to facilitate a precise historical understanding of early Christian texts and groups, all the more so since it can only lead to such broad generalizations as Klijn's, that early Christianity was a Jewish-Christian phenomenon" (Gerd Luedemann, *Opposition to Paul in Jewish Christianity*, trans. M. Eugene Boring [Minneapolis: Fortress Press, 1989], p. 29). Clearly, such error exists in regards to Abraham; the New Testament usage of Abraham is opposed to traditional and rabbinic usage of Abraham. For the early Christians, Abraham did not represent the everlasting covenant between God and Abraham's descendants, but rather, for early Christians, Abraham was claimed as a Christian, whose justifying faith in Christ is a model for regenerative faith.

[5] For instance, Saul of Tarsus could not become a priest because he was a Benjaminite, and he could not "join" the Sadducees, because they admitted only "priestly nobility and the rich patrician families" (Jerome Murphy-O'Connor, *Paul: His Story* [Oxford: Oxford University Press, 2004], p. 12). But since Pharisees were recruiting, they readily took in Saul of /Tarsus. The social environment of Jerusalem illustrates that Saul of Tarsus had limited possibilities for leadership within Judaism. And being a Pharisee did not really offer leadership opportunities, either. Murphy-O'Connor describes the plight of the Pharisees: "They had no power to impose their vision, so they strove continuously to influence the governing class by providing political support, and to win

right to be carriers of the Abrahamic tradition[6] or popular leaders[7] for that cause.[8] Thus, Abraham was made as the

---

the respect of the lower classes by clarifying the requirements of the Law in matters of daily domestic life" (p. 12).

[6] Murphy-O'Connor: "Why should Paul now take it for granted that Palestinian Jews would be hostile to him? I suspect that he was the victim of his gloomiest thoughts" (Murphy-O'Connor, p. 206). It is important to note that Murphy-O'Connor recognizes the fact that St. Paul considered himself to be in danger around Jews of Israel. This sentiment was not unfounded. In the summer of 56 AD, St. Paul was almost lynched by a non-Christian Jewish mob, and was saved from death when the Roman Tribune Claudius Lysias arrested St. Paul, away from the Jewish mob. Before Lysius began his torture, St. Paul claimed the rights of a Roman citizen (Acts 22:25). St. Paul wanted to be tried by the Roman procurator of Judais, Feli (52-58 AD), when Jewish authorities were insisting that St. Paul be handed over to them for judgment. Murphy-O'Connor describes this request by St. Paul: "What he wanted was for the procurator, the representative of Caesar, to make a decision in accordance with the evidence, and set him free. Festus, however, decided to interpret Paul's words as a demand to be judged in Rome by the emperor (Murphy-O'Connor, pp. 215-217). There was real conflict between Jewish leaders of Judaism and early Christian leaders that even involved lynching efforts and the manipulation of courts to obtain a conviction. But it was not only the non-Christian Jews who threatened St. Paul's life; "Christian" Jews also threatened St. Paul's life. Miurphy-O'Connor writes: "Once Paul became fully conscious of the threat posed by the Law, he forbade Jewish converts to circumcise their children and to observe the dietary laws. This ignited the anger of Jewish Christians who threatened his life on his last visit to Jerusalem. In the second and third centuries Jewish Christian vilification of Paul became systematic" (Murphy-O'Connor, p. 235). Luedemann agrees that Jewish Christians in Jerusalem took a decidedly anti-Paul position: "From the time of the conference, at the latest, the Jerusalem church assumed a preponderately anti-Pauline attitude" (Luedemann, p.61). That is why the Jerusalem Church refused the donation that St. Paul brought with him from Gentile Christians (Luedemann, pp. 60-62). The conflict between St. Paul and the Jews highlight the fact that there was a break between Christianity and Judaism at this time. Even if some Jewish converts to Christianity sided with the Jews, the distinctive conflict between Christianity and Judiasm cannot be gainsaid. Luedemann

Biblical Studies in Motion

Missing Link to justify Christianity in the New Testament. In this paper, I will show how St. Paul[9] illustrated Abraham as the Missing Link that provides the model of Christian faith that "justifies" the unbeliever who wants to become a Christian.

---

writes regarding the arrest of St. Paul by the Romans, which rescued him from death: "Thereby the stage is set for the following apologetic speeches by Paul, which place all the blame in the quarrel between Christians and Jews on the latter and urgently commend Christianity to the Romans" (Luedemann, p. 55). Certainly, early Christianity established its identity primary in opposition to Judaism and Jewish interpretation of the Old Testament. Further supporting the concept that there was a decided break between Christianity and Judaism is that despite the fact that the Jerusalem Church sided with the Jews against St. Paul, the leaders of the Jerusalem Church were ironically executed via stoning to death in 62 AD by the Jewish Sanhedrin, which charged James and other leaders of the Jerusalem Church with the violation of the Jewish Law (Luedemann, p. 62).

[7] It is important to recognize that Jerusalem leaders did not disagree with St. Paul's anti-Jewish animus, since they themselves were marginalized by legitimate Jewish authorities. Jerry L. Sumney regarding the summation of his research: "This study concludes that the evidence of the Pauline letters does not support the notion that the Christianity based in Jerusalem defined itself to any significant extent by opposition to Paul or the Pauline mission" (Jerry L. Sumney, *'Servants of Satan', 'False Brothers' and Other Opponents of Paul* [Sheffield: Sheffield Academic Press, 1999], p. 32).

[8] Francis Watson states: "The social reality which underlies Paul's discussions of Judaism and the law is his creation of Gentile Christian communities in sharp separation from the Jewish community. His theological reflection legitimates the separation of church from synagogue" (Francis Watson, *Paul, Judaism and the Gentiles: A Sociological Approach* [Cambridge: Cambridge University Press, 1986], p. 19).

[9] Luedemann writes: "The rumor described in Acts 21:21: the Pauline preaching means the destruction of Judaism..." (Luedemann, p. 61).

Biblical Studies in Motion

The New Testament can be seen as anti-Jewish in its texture and theme.[10] Jesus of Nazareth calls Jews, "Children of the Devil,"[11] in the Gospel of John (8:44). And St. Paul[12] wrote the Book of Galatians to emphasize that all Jewish forms must be abandoned by Jews who convert to Christianity.[13] The whole of the New Testament

---

[10] John G. Gager writes: "First, Paul has long been regarded as the source for Christian hatred of Jews and Judaism. Second, among Jews he has been the most hated of all Christians" (John G. Gager, *Reinventing Paul* [New York: Oxford University Press, 2000], p. 4). Gager further writes: "For the New Testament and certainly for those who created it, Paul was *the* theologian of Christian anti-Judaism, the rejection-replacement view of Judaism. Virtually all later readers – Christian, Jewish, and other – have assumed that Paul stands behind the anti-Judaism of the New Testament and mainstream Christianity" (Gager, p. 14).

[11] Watson states: "In [John] 8:44 it is said that their father is the devil, and that they carry out his desires. …. The sectarian character of the Johannine community is thus seen in its undifferentiated hostility towards the Jewish community as a whole, and not just towards its leaders. Leaders and people alike are denounced" (Watson, p. 44).

[12] W. D. Davies states: "Recently the charge has been made that Paul was an anti-Semite. Outside Romans 11, anti-Semitism emerges implicitly, it is urged, in his broad interpretation of the Christian life as involving a radical break with Judaism, which it has to leave behind. Inside Romans 11 it emerges explicitly. There Paul's program for the future and for Israel's role in it, which leads to the ultimate desired disappearance of Jews in the church or their absorption by the church, unmasks his anti-Semitism" (W. D. Davies, *Jewish and Pauline Studies*[Philadelphia: Fortress Press, 1984], p. 134).

[13] Walter Brueggemann describes the sentiment of the Jews regarding God's covenantal blessing: "Israel is certain, for all time to come, that this God does not want this people to live without a secure land" (Walter Brueggemann, *Theology of the Old Testament: Testimony, Dispute, Advocacy* [Minneapolis: Fortress Press, 1997], p. 169). The early Christian, by in large, did not agree that God's covenantal promise continued with the Jews; rather, it was the new covenant which blessed the followers of Jesus Christ.

has an anti-Jewish texture.[14] This anti-Jewish animus of the New Testament has been recognized by both Jews and Christians[15] throughout two thousand years[16] of western history since the birth of Jesus of Nazareth in Bethlehem.

There are several causes for the strong anti-Jewish spirit in the New Testament. Certainly, among the most prominent reasons is the fact that Jews and Judaism

---

[14] Peter Tomson writes: "A study of Paul's Jewish antecedents reveals his indebtedness to the teacher of Nazareth. This may seem disconcerting to the guardias of academic and ecclesiastical theology, but it is a relief to those who wish to follow Jesus" (Peter J. Tomson, *Paul and the Jewish Law: Halakha in the Letters of the Apostle to the Gentiles* [Assen/Maastricht: Van Gorcum, 1990], p. xiv).

[15] E. P. Sanders states that St. Paul directly attacks Judaism in "the traditional understanding of the covenant and election" (E. P. Sanders, *Paul, the Law and the Jewish People* [Philadelphia: Fortress Press, 1983], p. 46). Francis Watson writes: "What is the nature of Paul's attack on Judaism and Judaizing Christianity? It is increasingly being recognized by New Testament scholars that the answer to this question can no longer be taken for granted" (Watson, p. 1). F. C. Bauer, the father of modern Pauline studies, attacked Jewish exclusivism, and Lutherans have traditionally criticized "the Jewish attempt to earn salvation" (Watson, p. 12). Bauer emphasized that the early Christian church was "dominated by the conflict between Jewish Christianity, represented by James, and Pauline Gentile Christianity" (Watson, p. 12). Thus, St. Paul's attack of Jews included Jews who converted to Christianity, but were not willing to abandon forms and practices of Judaism.

[16] Sidney G. Hall III states: "For nearly two thousand years Christians have espoused a theology of anti-Judaism. Since at least the latter half of the first century, Christians embraced a theology of rejection and replacement of the Jewish people. Anti-Jewish theology has been a principal doctrine of Christianity from early Gentile Christians to Irenaeus, from Augustine to Martin Luther, from Adolf von Harnack to Gerhard Kittel, Paul Tillich, and many contemporary theologians" (Sidney G. Hall III, *Christian Anti-Semitism and Paul's Theology* [Minneapolis: Fortress Press, 1993], p. ix-x).

rejected[17] Jesus of Nazareth and his followers, as shown by St. Stephen's speech in Acts 7 (see also, I Thessalonians 2:14-16). The four Gospel books clearly implicate Jews in a conspiracy to kill Jesus of Nazareth (Matt. 5:12, 23:29-39; Luke 11:47-51), as shown in the Passion Narratives. The conspiracy is not only intentional, but it also involves the highest members of the legitimate ruling body of the Jews at that time. The Gospel of John records Caiaphas, the High Priest of the Jerusalem Temple, who was also the head of the Sanhedrin, which is equivalent to the US Senate or the UK Parliament, making the statement that it is better to have Jesus of Nazareth killed than jeopardize the Jewish population (John 11:49-50). The legitimate Jewish government authorities perceived Jesus of Nazareth as a threat to the Jewish state of Israel. The systematic program to assassinate Jesus of Nazareth failed on a few occasions, and a more formal route to having Jesus of Nazareth killed was pursued through the court system. The four Gospels record the Jews[18] being successful in their endeavor to have Jesus of Nazareth executed.[19]

---

[17] Watson writes: "Here at last we are on solid ground in our investigation of the origins of the Gentile mission: it began in response to Jewish failure to believe the gospel. Who was responsible for this momentous decision to turn to the Gentiles? Gal. 2 provides the answer: it was Paul, Barnabas and the other Jewish Christians at Antioch" (Watson, p. 32).

[18] W. D. Davies states: "The claims that Jews had crucified Jesus and murdered the prophets cannot be neatly postponed to a date after the fall of Jerusalem" (W. D. Davies, p. 125).

[19] Tomson points to the aggressive anti-Judaism of Jesus Christ: "Jesus was a Jew, but one who fundamentally criticized Judaism and especially the Law. In order to make this plausible, a conceptual model was needed which could describe Jewish religious life as the ideological antipode of Jesus' message" (Tomson, p. 5).

Biblical Studies in Motion

Besides the direct attack on Jesus of Nazareth himself, the Jews and Jewish authorities are described in the New Testament tradition as intentionally hunting down Christians. St. Paul himself stands as an example of a Jewish agent sent by legitimate Jewish authorities to hunt down and arrest Christians before his own conversion to Christianity (Acts 9:1-2). The Gospel of John (9:22; 16:2) records a verdict by Jewish authorities to expel Jews who have converted to Christianity from the synagogues.[20] In other words, legitimate Jewish authorities criminalized following Jesus of Nazareth and prevented Jews who followed him from participating in Jewish religious and cultural activities. Francis Watson describes this as the consequence of Jewish rejection of Jesus:

> The suffering of the community at the hands of the Jews is not to disturb its members, since it is the logical consequence of the Jews' hostility towards Jesus himself (15:18-21). This tendency to explain suffering by tracing it back to Jewish hostility towards Jesus accounts for the fact that the expulsion from the synagogue experienced by the Johannine community

---

[20] Watson states: "Christian missionaries had already been alienated from the synagogue by Jewish rejection of their message, and the Gentile mission set the seal on that alienation, for the abandonment of essential parts of the law of Moses would have been quite incompatible with continuing membership of the synagogue" (Watson, p. 36). Even during the time of the Jesus movement, followers of Jesus of Nazareth went out on missionary activity to Jewish towns, but were often rejected. Leaders of Jewish synagogues had a particular problem with Jesus of Nazareth teaching against Jewish laws, as evidenced in the Sermon on the Mount ("You have heard it said, but I say unto you…") and Jesus of Nazareth's teaching on divorce.

(16:2) is retrojected into the earthly life of Jesus in 9:22, 34 and 12:42.[21]

The Jewish documents themselves confirm this decision against Christ-followers in the Eighteen Benedictions, which calls for the excommunication of the "Nazarenes," or those who follow Jesus of Nazareth. Thus, Jewish converts to Christianity were deprived of hereditary rights to be leaders of Jewish communities in any way. It is, therefore, not surprising that the followers of Jesus of Nazareth preserved and pushed an aggressively anti-Jewish agenda in the early Christian movement. It was not in their interest to prop up the Abrahamic covenant, which *de facto* excluded the early Christian leaders, even those who came from Jewish background.

Thus, the former Pharisee[22] St. Paul and the rest of the early Christian leaders, even many who were from Jewish backgrounds, espoused an aggressive new identity in Christ Jesus, apart from the Old Covenant between God and Abraham. W. D. Davies states: "Paul redefined the law and Israel in terms of Jesus the Messiah."[23] For the early Christians, the Old Covenant was nullified[24] through

---

[21] Watson, p. 43.

[22] Timo Laato states that St. Paul "mentions his Pharisee past as a warning example in Phil. 3:4-9, [and] his criticism is finally applied to Judaism in general" (Timo Laato, *Paul and Judaism: An Anthropological Approach*, trans. T. McElwain [Atlanta: Scholars Press, 1995], p. 3).

[23] Davies, p. 124.

[24] Elias Bickerman emphasizes the conditional nature of divine covenant with Israel. Bickerman argues that God acts out of divine wrath when the covenant obligations are violated. An example Bickerman provides is the "covenant" obligation to observe the Sabbath Day as found in Jeremiah 17:19-27. Bickerman argues that

Jewish rejection and murder of Jesus Christ, and the New Covenant was in place. Obviously, it was Jesus of Nazareth who used the terminology of the New Covenant in the Lord's Supper, which early Christians celebrated as the Eucharist, a tradition which has continued without a break until the current time. For the early Christians, there was a new covenant in place that has replaced the Old Covenant made between God and Abraham. The New Covenant was the covenant in the blood of Jesus of Nazareth.

Interestingly enough, the baby was not thrown out with the bath water. Although the Old Covenant between God and Abraham was dismissed as null and void and the New Covenant in Christ's blood was set in its place, early Christians still revered Abraham and tried to claim him as their own. This practice started with the Jesus tradition. Jesus of Nazareth emphasized that Abraham had faith in

---

like other covenants, violation necessarily brings down the wrathful judgement of God upon Israel. Bickerman writes: "Les Juifs, en violant le repos sabbatique, transportent des fardeaux le jour du Sabbat par les portes de Jérusalem. Donc, Dieu mettra le feu à ces portes; il dévorera les palais de Jérusalem et ne s'éteindra pas. Comme le *berith* de Sédécias a été conclue 'devant' Dieu, et dans le Temple qui porte son nom (vv. 15, 18), les violateurs de 'sa' *berith*seront châtiés par la divinité outragée" (Elias Bickerman, *Studies in Jewish and Christian History* [Leiden: E. J. Brill, 1976], pp. 5-6). Thus, Bickerman shows that there was an adverse divine response to covenant-breakers built into all "covenant" God made with Israel. For the early Christians, the Jewish rejection of Jesus of Nazareth as the messiah as a people explains why God acted with wrath towards the Jewish people. Bickerman describes the covenant between God and Israel as similar to God's demand upon Israel to keep the law of God. When God gives the law of God, the Israelites have the choice to live by observing it or die by violating it. Bickerman writes: "L'orateur place Israël devant l'alternative: la vie avec le bien ou la mort avec le mal (Deut. XXX, 15)" (Bickerman, p. 28).

him (John 8:39). This statement angered the Jews, who saw Jesus of Nazareth before them. Claiming that Jesus of Nazareth was blaspheming in pointing to his nature as divine by claiming that he existed during the time of Abraham, Jews sought to kill Jesus of Nazareth (John 8:56-59). In the same manner that Jesus of Nazareth claimed Abraham for Christianity, the Gospel writers claimed Abraham as their own. One way that the Gospel writers claimed Abraham as their own was by disavowing the descendants of Abraham as the children of God. John the Baptizer preaches that Abraham's descendants were unnecessary because God could make stones into "Abraham's children" (Matthew 3:9). Furthermore, the Gospel of John claims that Abraham's children are not the children of God, but rather those who had faith in Jesus Christ (John 1:12-13). In other words, Jews were not Abraham's descendants, but rather it was Christians with the same faith that Abraham had in Jesus of Nazareth. For these early Christians, Abraham was the Missing Link that linked the Old Testament with the New Testament. Because of the faith of Abraham, it could be argued that it was faith in Christ Jesus that those in the Old Testament were saved or "justified," just like those in the New Testament. Thus, Abraham was the Missing Link to justify Christianity in the New Testament.

In keeping with the Gospel tradition, St. Paul illustrates Abraham as the Missing Link[25] that provides the

---

[25] John G. Gager states: "Abraham is the scriptural guarantor of Paul's gospel to and about the Gentiles. Here again, Paul stands in a long line of Jewish thinkers, beginning with the book of Genesis, who see Abraham as the key to understanding the ultimate salvation of Gentiles" (Gager, p. 123).

model of Christian faith that "justifies" the unbeliever who wants to become a Christian. For St. Paul, Abraham was not important as the ancestor of Jews,[26] but as a father of

---

[26] This is in sharp contrast to the way the Jews viewed the Abrahamic covenant. John Van Seters describes the Abrahamic covenant as necessarily tied to biological descendants of Abraham and to the Jewish ownership of the land of Palestine. This understanding was assumed within the Old Testament tradition and by Jews. Van Seters writes: "The subject of inheritance leads first to the divine promise of numerous progeny and then to the promise of inheritance/possession of the land. So closely are these two themes intertwined that it has been a mistake in the past for scholars to try to separate them" (John Van Seters, *Prologue to History: The Yahwist as Historian in Genesis* [Louisville: Westminster/John Knox Press, 1992], p. 250). Nahum Sarna also agrees and emphasizes seeing the promise of land and posterity together; however, Sarna emphasizes the promise of posterity as preceding the promise of the land, logically. Sarna writes regarding Genesis 15: "The bipartite blessing of great posterity and of possession of the land is, as in chapter 12, separated into its individual components, save that the promise of national territory presupposes the existence of a people, and therefore incorporates also the blessing of offspring" (Nahum M. Sarna, *Understanding Genesis* [New York: The Jewish Theological Seminary of America, 1966], p. 120). Walther Eichrodt describes the sociological function of the covenant for the Israelites: "That which unites the tribes to one another and makes them a unified people with a strong sense of solidarity is the will of God. It is in the name of Yahweh and in the covenant sanctioned by him that the tribes find the unifying bond, which proves a match even for the centrifugal tendencies of tribal egoism and creates from highly diversified elements a whole with a common law, a common cultus and a common historical consciousness" (Walther Eichrodt, *Theology of the Old Testament: Volume One* [Philadelphia: The Westminster Press, 1961], p. 39). Van Seters, Eichrodt, and Sarna, in effect, highlight the radical nature of the New Testament and the interpretation of the Abrahamic covenant offered by St. Paul. Early Christians were interested in wiping Jews out of the book of the covenant. However, Van Seter notes that other parts of the Old Testament emphasized the conditional nature of the Abrahamic covenant. Van Seter writes: "The descendants of Abraham, 'the many," are making unconditional claims to the land through their forefather. But this is opposed by Ezekiel on the basis, as in the Dtr tradition, that possession of the land is

faith in Jesus Christ[27]; this is clearly evident in the Book of Galatians. St. Paul argues that those who have faith are Abraham's children (Galatians 3:7). Furthermore, St. Paul emphasizes that Abraham was justified by faith (Galatians 3:6). James Dunn notes that it is unclear whether St. Paul or his opponents brought in Abraham in Galatians 3:15-18, but the introduction of Abraham brought the discussion of circumcision to the centerpiece of debate.[28] Sumney argues that Paul brings Abraham into the argument.[29] Whether St. Paul introduced Abraham or not, it is significant that St. Paul in Galatians 3:16 argues for the exclusion of descendants of Abraham as the inheritors of the covenant

---

conditional, even though this position is formulated in Ezekiel's own language" (Van Seters, p. 250). Thus, Van Seters illustrates that even from the Old Testament, the rejection of the Jews and their exclusion from the covenant was foreshadowed. In fact, Van Seter shows that justification, or righteousness, was essential to the covenantal blessing. Van Seters writes: "What is the relationship of God's declaration of righteousness (v. 6) and the possession of the land? As we noted above in Ezek. 33:24ff., the prophet declares that without righteousness there can be no claim to possession of the land. This is clearly the heritage of the Dtr land-theology" (Van Seters, pp. 250-251). Eichrodt also emphasize the genetic connection to Abraham was irrelevant; he argues that the Old Testament emphasized faith in God for justification. Eichrodt writes: "Moreover, the decisive requirement for admission is not natural kinship but readiness to submit oneself to the will of the divine Lord of the Covenant and to vow oneself to this particular God" (Eichrodt, p. 39). Thus, Eichrodt, li,e Van Seters, show that St. Paul's rhetoric was anticipated in the Old Testament.

[27] Hall states: "Paul bridges the story of Abraham and Sarah to the story of Christ. The Christ-event is the fulfillment of the Abrahamic promise. The promise is not new to Gentiles, but they are now made fully aware of it, apart from the law, through the death and resurrection of Christ" (Hall, p. 85).

[28] James D. G. Dunn, *A Commentary on the Epistle to the Galatians* (London: A. & C. Black, 1993), p. 16.

[29] Sumney, p. 155.

between God and Abraham.³⁰ St. Paul states that the Abrahamic covenant was given to Abraham and his "seed" in the singular and not to Abraham's "seeds" in the plural. And, the seed referred to in the Book of Genesis is Jesus Christ.³¹

The fact that St. Paul reinterprets the traditionally understood Abrahamic covenant is significant. Traditionally, the Abrahamic covenant was understood to be given to Abraham and the physical descendants of Abraham. It was based on this notion that the Jews argued that the Jews were the children of the covenant. However, St. Paul annuls the traditional understanding of the Abrahamic covenant as being applicable to the Jews in any shape or form.³² For St. Paul, the Abrahamic covenant was given to Abraham and his "seed" who is Jesus Christ. Thus, all the Jews are excluded from the Abrahamic covenant.³³ This argument of St. Paul is akin to arguing that the Abrahamic covenant is not valid for the Jews based on their identity. The significant emphasis is that St. Paul argues that the Abrahamic covenant was never intended for the Jews in the first place. The reason that a former Pharisee

---

³⁰ Watson states: "Paul disinherits the Jewish community and claims that his congregations of mainly Gentile Christians are the sole legitimate possessors of these traditions" (Watson, p. 70).

³¹ Davies also includes "those baptiaed into him" as the true seed along with Christ (Davies, p. 127).

³² Davies states: "The meaning of 'descent' from Abraham has to be radically reconsidered: it no longer has a 'physical' connotation. Christian believers are the sons and daughters of God' they can now cry 'Abba' and are the heirs of the promise to Abraham" (Davies, p. 128).

³³ Watson states: "Paul claims simply that as God's way of salvation is through faith in Christ, Judaism is automatically disqualified" (Watson, p. 17).

argues in this manner about the Abrahamic covenant can be attributed to St. Paul's Christ experience which completely changed his life; he became more aggressively anti-Jewish than other apostles. In essence, St. Paul used Abraham as a weapon against his Jewish opponents. Sumney writes: "Abraham is Paul's evidence against the opponents, not the opponents' evidence for their position."[34]

This is also poignantly evident in Romans 4. St. Paul makes the clear point that Abrahamic covenant did not play a role in Abraham's justification.[35] In Romans 4:10-11a, St. Paul writes: "Under what circumstances was it credited? Was it after he was circumcised, or before? It was not after, but before! And he received the sign of circumcision, a seal of the righteousness that he had by faith while he was still uncircumcised" (NIV). It is clear here that St. Paul negates the value of circumcision, and thereby the Abrahamic covenant itself. Circumcision was a mere sign[36] of Abraham's justification and did not play any role in Abraham's justification. This represents an opposition to the traditional Jewish understanding of

---

[34] Sumney, p. 156.

[35] This is particularly significant in light of the fact that Jewish Christians were the primary audience for Romans. Watson writes: "Romans was not addressed exclusively to Jewish Christians, even though its content suggests that they are the primary addressees" (p. 104). In fact, Watson argues that St. Paul used Romans to "persuade them to make a final break with the Jewish community" (p. 106).

[36] Robert Jewett states: "In place of circumcision as a 'sign of the covenant,' which would retain the premise of Israel's preeminent position as Yahweh's sole covenant partner, Paul speaks of circumcision as the sign of something else, that is, the 'righteousness through faith' that was ascribed to Abraham while he was still an uncircumcised Gentile" (Robert Jewett, *Romans: A Commentary* [Minneapolis: Fortress Press, 2007], p. 319).

circumcision as an integral part of the covenant itself.[37] St. Paul's intention to negate the exclusive claims[38] of the Abrahamic covenant is clear in his following statement in Romans 4:11b: "So then, he is the father of all who believe but have not been circumcised, in order that righteousness might be credited to them" (NIV). St. Paul makes it clear here that circumcision is unnecessary for justification.[39] It is only through faith that one is justified. Brendan Byrne writes:

> In claiming Abraham for faith in this sense Paul swims against the prevailing current. The post-biblical Jewish tradition, while basically preserving the sense of Abraham as the one who received God's covenant on behalf of Israel, also laid considerable stress upon the patriarch as a figure of obedience and trust. His acceptance of the divine ordinance concerning circumcision was held to be a kind of anticipatory fulfillment of the Torah.[40]

---

[37] Robert Jewett argues that Abraham was a hero for the Jews who held him up as the model of Jewish law observance as indicated in Jewish writings, such as Sirach, extant at St. Paul's time (Jewett, p. 309). In this light, St. Paul can be seen as attacking the heart of Judaism.

[38] Watson states that St. Paul "opposes the view that Abraham legitimates the way of life of the loyal and faithful Jew who observes the law, and he opposes the view that that the promise to Abraham gives grounds for the hope of salvation for those who are his physical descendants. He thus attacks vital elements in the self-understanding of the Jewish community" (Watson, p. 138).

[39] Robert Jewett writes: "The formula remains odd for Abraham, who is depicted here as the honorific parent of all believers, explicitly including those unconnected to his physical lineage" (Jewett. p. 307).

[40] Brendan Byrne, *Romans* (Collegeville: The Liturgical Press, 1996), p. 142.

Douglas Moo agrees and adds that St. Paul was arguing not only with Jews but also with Jewish Christians who held onto Jewishness. Moo states:

> But why has Paul singled out Abraham as the reference point for this expansion? One reason is undoubtedly polemical. Abraham was revered by the Jews as their 'father' and his life and character were held up as models of God's ways with his people and of true piety. .... Paul would naturally show his Roman readers that this understanding of Abraham, which his Jewish and Jewish-Christian opponents undoubtedly cited against his teaching (cf. Gal. 3-4), was not in accord with the OT. Through Paul's interpretation of Gen. 15:6, Abraham is wrested from the Jews as an exemplar of torah-obedience and made into an exemplar of faith.[41]

In essence, St. Paul uses Abraham as the Missing Link to justify Christianity as the true religion and, in effect, to show Judaism as a false religion.[42]

---

[41] Douglas J. Moo, *The Epistle to the Romans* (Grand Rapids: William B. Eerdmans Publishing Company, 1996), p. 256.

[42] Robert Jewett writes: "This option also produces an egregious conflict with Paul's later argument that Abraham's 'children of the promise' rather than his 'fleshly children' are the legitimate 'children of God' (9:9)" (Jewett, p. 307). However, Jewett does not need to see a conflict, here. Romans 4 and Romans 9 agree that it is essentially faith that justifies; in other words, it is those with faith, or the New Covenant and the new promise, who are the true children of God. St. Paul writes

For St. Paul, Abraham, in essence, was a Christian and the father of Christians. N. T. Wright describes the integral connection between Abraham and Christianity in the ideas of St. Paul in Romans 4: "It goes with his whole theology, to which we shall turn presently, of how God's intention in the beginning of creation itself is now fulfilled through Christ and the Spirit, and how this was likewise God's intention when he called Abraham."[43] St. Paul emphasizes the requirements of Christian faith for Jews who want to be justified.[44] St. Paul writes in Romans 4:12: "And he is also the father of the circumcised who not only are circumcised but who also walk in the footsteps of the faith that our father Abraham had before he was

---

in Romans 9:31-32: "But Israel, who pursued a law of righteousness, has not attained it. Why not? Because they pursued it not by faith but as if it were by works. They stumbled over the 'stumbling stone'" (NIV).

[43] N. T. Wright, "New Exodus, New Inheritance: The Narrative Substructure of Romans 3-8," *Romans and the People of God: Essays in Honor of Gordon D. Fee on the Occasion of His 65th Birthday*, eds. Sven K. Soderlund and N. T. Wright (Grand Rapids: William B. Eerdmans Publishing Company, 1999, pp. 26-35), p. 3.

[44] Robert Jewett states: "The correspondence between Christ believers and Abraham continues by referring to them as 'those having faith in the one who raised Jesus our Lord from the dead'" (Jewett, p. 341). Jewett explains: "As Paul explains in detail elsewhere (1 Cor 15), and assumes that every believer understands, the starting point of faith in Christ is faith in his resurrection. If the Crucified One had not been resurrected, there would have been no proof that he was indeed the Messiah" (Jewett, p. 342). N. T. Wright agrees that Christ's resurrection is pivotal to Christ's messianic work: "It is that through which God has broken in to the world and to the sorry history of Israel, unveiling his faithfulness in a radically new way in the death and resurrection of the Messiah and the outpouring of the Spirit" (Wright, p. 33). Furthermore, Brendan Byrne notes that Christ's resurrection was a paradigm for the future resurrection of Christian believers in the conceptualization of the Christ-event by St. Paul (Byrne, p. 155).

circumcised" (NIV). In this statement, St. Paul essentially disowns the Jews who are circumcised but do not have faith in Jesus Christ.[45] For St. Paul, it was only the faith in Jesus Christ that justified. Even Abraham was justified by faith in Jesus Christ, and so Jews in St. Paul's time must have faith in Jesus Christ or they would not be saved. In other words, circumcision was useless. Thus, the Abrahamic covenant for the Jews was useless. St. Paul encapsulates the salvation formula in Romans 4:23-25: "The words 'it was credited to him' were not written for him alone, but also for us, to whom God will credit righteousness – for us who believe in him who raised Jesus our Lord from the dead. He was delivered over to death for our sins and was raised to life for our justification" (NIV). For St. Paul, salvation, or justification, was only possible through faith in Jesus Christ. Believing in God means to believe in Jesus Christ – in his death and in his resurrection. Thus, for St. Paul, Abraham is the Missing Link in the Bible that connects the Old Testament and the New Testament, together.

It is not surprising why many incendiary attacks have been leveled against St. Paul the Apostle. St. Paul opposed the traditional Jewish emphasis that Jews were the People of God. Furthermore, St. Paul excised the necessary connection between the Jews and Abraham. In fact, St. Paul made Abraham a disciple of Jesus Christ. It is the radical Christ-centered interpretation of the Abrahamic Covenant and Abraham himself that caused many Jews to

---

[45] Watson states: "Paul abandoned his preaching to the Jews because he became convinced that God had hardened their hearts against the gospel" (Watson, p. 45).

hate St. Paul the Apostle for two thousand years. St. Paul had made Abraham the Missing Link to connect Christians to Abraham and to deny the Jews their birthright as descendants of Abraham.

Biblical Studies in Motion

Bibliography

Bickerman, Elias. *Studies in Jewish and Christian History*. Leiden: E. J. Brill, 1976.

Brueggemann, Walter. *Theology of the Old Testament: Testimony, Dispute, Advocacy.* Minneapolis: Fortress Press, 1997.

Byrne, Brendan. *Romans*. Collegeville: The Liturgical Press, 1996.

Davies, W. D. *Jewish and Pauline Studies*. Philadelphia: Fortress Press, 1984.

Gager, John G. *Reinventing Paul*. New York: Oxford University Press, 2000.

Eichrodt, Walther. *Theology of the Old Testament (Volume One)*. Translated by J. A. Baker. Philadelphia: The Westminster Press, 1961.

Hall, Sidney G., III. *Christian Anti-Semitism and Paul's Theology*. Minneapolis: Fortress Press, 1993.

Hays, Richard B. *Echoes of Scripture in the Letters of Paul*. New Haven: Yale University Press, 1989.

Jewett, Robert. *Romans: A Commentary*. Minneapolis: Fortress Press, 2007.

Laato, Timo. *Paul and Judaism: An Anthropological Approach.* Translated by T. McElwain. Atlanta: Scholars Press, 1995.

Moberly, R. W. L. *The Old Testament of the Old Testament.* Minneapolis: Fortress Press, 1992.

Moo, Douglas J. *The Epistle to the Romans.* Grand Rapids: William B. Eerdmans Publishing Company, 1996.

Murphy-O'Connor, Jerome. *Paul: His Story.* Oxford: Oxford University Press, 2004.

Luedemann, Gerd. *Opposition to Paul in Jewish Christianity.* Translated by M. Eugene Boring. Minneapolis: Fortress Press, 1989.

Sampley, J. Paul (Editor). *Paul in the Greco-Roman World: A Handbook.* Harrisburg: Trinity Press International, 2003.

Sanders, E. P. *Paul, the Law and the Jewish People.* Philadelphia: Fortress Press, 1983.

Sarna, Nahum M. *Understanding Genesis.* New York: The Jewish Theological Seminary of America, 1966.

Smith, Morton. *Palestinian Parties and Politics that Shaped the Old Testament.* London: SCM Press, 1987.

Soderlund, Sven K., and N. T. Wright (Editors). *Romans and the People of God: Essays in Honor of Gordon D. Fee on the Occasion of His 65th Birthday*. Grand Rapids: William B. Eerdmans Publishing Company, 1999.

Stanley, Christopher D. *Paul and the Language of Scripture: Citation Technique in the Pauline Epistles and Contemporary Literature*. Cambridge: Cambridge University Press, 1992.

Sumney, Jerry L. *'Servants of Satan', 'False Brothers' and Other Opponents of Paul*. Sheffield: Sheffield Academic Press, 1999.

Tomson, Peter J. *Paul and the Jewish Law: Halakha in the Letters of the Apostle to the Gentiles*. Assen/Maastricht: Van Gorcum, 1990.

Van Seters, John. *Prologue to History: The Yahwist as Historian in Genesis*. Louisville: Westminster/John Knox Press, 1992.

Von Rad, Gerhard. *Genesis: A Commentary*. Philadelphia: Fortress Press, 1972.

Watson, Francis. *Paul, Judaism and the Gentiles: A Sociological Approach*. Cambridge: Cambridge University Press, 1986.

Yinger, Kent L. *Paul, Judaism, and Judgment According to Deeds*. Cambridge: Cambridge University Press, 1999.

www.ingramcontent.com/pod-product-compliance
Lightning Source LLC
Chambersburg PA
CBHW030234240426
43663CB00036B/438